ProductID: ACCUPLACERFlash

ACCUPLACER
Exam

D0888381

Flashcard Study System

MOMETRIX
TEST PREPARATION

Flashcard Study System

"Get the help you need to ace your test today.

Guaranteed results!"

e World's Most Comprehensive Test Preparation Company™

· Co
· Tea
· Med
· Insu
· Finan
Exam
Gradu
Scho

Flashcard Study System

Over 1000 different standardized exams

GUARANTEED IMPROVE YOUR SCORE

Flashcard Study Sy

· Effective
· Affordable
· Guaranteed

ISBN 978-1-60971-017-0

90000

9 781609 710170

Easy-to-separate, perforated flashcards enclosed.

Thank you for your purchasing Mometrix flashcards!

We appreciate you entrusting your test preparation to us and take this responsibility very seriously. We have painstakingly reviewed piles of content and boiled it all down to the most critical information most likely to be on the exam. Your diligent use of these flashcards will help you get the results you want.

As you start reviewing these flashcards, you might think, "Wow! That sure is a lot of information." and it may seem a bit overwhelming at first. We have intentionally packed each flashcard with a lot of information to help you truly understand the critical concepts over which your test questions are based. Here's a little secret that you are probably already aware of: test-makers intentionally try to trip you up by the way they word the questions. The reason they do this is to make sure the test-taker truly understands the information and didn't just memorize it. We have designed these flashcards to help you fully understand each concept so you can get the answers right regardless of how the questions are worded on the test.

The "Leitner Method" of Studying Flashcards for Maximum Learning in Minimum Time

In the 1970's, a German psychologist named Sebastian Leitner developed a "learning machine" using flashcards that can supercharge your success by using the power of prioritization and positive feedback. This approach to using flashcards maximizes your time and makes studying more like a game.

Here's how his system works. Take three separate shoeboxes or divide one shoebox into three parts using some type of divider and label the sections or boxes with a 1, 2 or 3 (you could do as many as six boxes if you prefer). You start the "game" by placing all of the cards into the first box or section. As you go through the flashcard deck for the first time, place any cards you answer correctly into the next section, in this case Box 2. Study any you miss as you go through the cards, but any you miss go in Box 1. In your next study session, study the cards in Box 2 only and move any you miss back to Box 1 and any you answer correctly to Box 3. Repeat until you have as many cards as you can in the last box. Then you should have two stacks: one in the last box consisting of cards you have answered correctly at least twice, and one in the first box of cards you have missed at least once. Repeat this whole process until you have moved the entire deck into the last box.

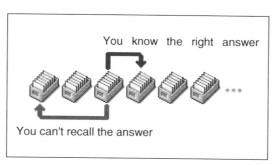

Research shows that at least 3 repetitions are necessary to guarantee memory retention beyond short-term. To maximize your advantage, use the system in the weeks approaching the exam to train your long-term memory, then study the entire deck again the day of the exam to train your short-term memory.

From all of us here at Mometrix, we wish you the best of luck on your exam!

How to Access Your Free Bonus Material
For your convenience, we have made your free bonus material accessible online at:
http://www.mometrix.com/bonus948/accuplacer

Need more help?
Check out our study guides at: http://MometrixStudyGuides.com/ACCUPLACER

Explain how to find the greatest common factor of a group of algebraic expressions.

Differentiate between *mean* and *weighted mean*.

Describe *monomials* and *polynomials*.

Identify patterns of special products: *perfect trinomial squares*, the *difference between two squares*, the *sum and difference of two cubes*, and *perfect cubes*.

Explain how to multiply two binomials.

Describe the process of dividing polynomials.

Mean: The same thing as the arithmetic average. Use the formula

$$\text{mean} = \frac{\text{sum of all numbers in the set}}{\text{quantity of numbers in the set}}$$

Weighted mean: Weighted values, such as $w_1, w_2, w_3, \ldots$ are assigned to each member of the set $x_1, x_2, x_3, \ldots$. Use the formula

$$\text{weighted mean} = \frac{w_1 x_1 + w_2 x_2 + w_3 x_3 + \cdots + w_n x_n}{w_1 + w_2 + w_3 + \cdots + w_n}$$

Make sure there is one weighted value for each member of the set.

The greatest common factor of a group of algebraic expressions may be a monomial or a polynomial. Begin by factoring all the algebraic expressions until each expression is represented as a group of factors consisting of monomials and prime polynomials. To find the greatest common factor, take each monomial or polynomial that appear as a factor in every algebraic expression and multiply. This will give you a polynomial with the largest numerical coefficient and largest degree that is a factor of the given algebraic expressions.

Perfect Trinomial Squares: $x^2 + 2xy + y^2 = (x + y)^2$ or
$$x^2 - 2xy + y^2 = (x - y)^2$$
Difference Between Two Squares: $x^2 - y^2 = (x + y)(x - y)$
Sum of Two Cubes: $x^3 + y^3 = (x + y)(x^2 - xy + y^2)$
Note: the second factor is NOT the same as a perfect trinomial square, so do not try to factor it further.
Difference Between Two Cubes: $x^3 - y^3 = (x - y)(x^2 + xy + y^2)$
Again, the second factor is NOT the same as a perfect trinomial square.
Perfect Cubes: $x^3 + 3x^2y + 3xy^2 + y^3 = (x + y)^3$ and
$$x^3 - 3x^2y + 3xy^2 - y^3 = (x - y)^3$$

Monomial: A single constant, variable, or product of constants and variables, such as 2, x, $2x$, or $\frac{2}{x}$. There will never be addition or subtraction symbols in a monomial. Like monomials have like variables, but they may have different coefficients.
Polynomial: An algebraic expression which uses addition and subtraction to combine two or more monomials. Two terms make a binomial; three terms make a trinomial.
Degree of a Monomial: The sum of the exponents of the variables.
Degree of a Polynomial: The highest degree of any individual term.

Set up a long division problem, dividing a polynomial by either a monomial or another polynomial of equal or lesser degree. When dividing by a monomial, divide each term of the polynomial by the monomial.
When dividing a polynomial by a polynomial, begin by arranging the terms of each polynomial in order of one variable. You may arrange in ascending or descending order, but be consistent with both polynomials. To get the first term of the quotient, divide the first term of the dividend by the first term of the divisor. Multiply the first term of the quotient by the entire divisor and subtract that product from the dividend. Repeat for the second and successive terms until you either get a remainder of zero or a remainder whose degree is less than the degree of the divisor. If the quotient has a remainder, write the answer as a mixed expression in the form

$\text{quotient} + \frac{\text{remainder}}{\text{divisor}}$.

First: Multiply the first term of each binomial
Outer: Multiply the outer terms of the binomials
Inner: Multiply the inner terms of the binomials
Last: Multiply the last term of each binomial
$$(Ax + By)(Cx + Dy) = ACx^2 + ADxy + BCxy + BDy^2$$

Explain how to factor a polynomial.

Describe *rational expressions*.

Explain *complex fractions*.

Discuss the terms *one variable linear equation*, *root*, *solution set*, *empty set*, and *equivalent equations* as they relate to equations.

Explain how to solve one-variable linear equations.

Explain *absolute value*.

Rational Expression. A fraction with polynomials in both the numerator and the denominator; the value of the polynomial in the denominator cannot be equal to zero.

To add or subtract rational expressions, first find the common denominator, then rewrite each fraction as an equivalent fraction with the common denominator. Finally, add or subtract the numerators to get the numerator of the answer, and keep the common denominator as the denominator of the answer.

When multiplying rational expressions, factor each polynomial and cancel like factors (a factor which appears in both the numerator and the denominator). Then, multiply all remaining factors in the numerator to get the numerator of the product, and multiply the remaining factors in the denominator to get the denominator of the product. Remember – cancel entire factors, not individual terms.

To divide rational expressions, take the reciprocal of the divisor (the rational expression you are dividing by) and multiply by the dividend.

First, check for a common monomial factor. When the greatest common monomial factor has been factored out, look for patterns of special products: differences of two squares, the sum or difference of two cubes for binomial factors, or perfect trinomial squares for trinomial factors. If the factor is a trinomial but not a perfect trinomial square, look for a factorable form, such as

$$x^2 + (a + b)x + ab = (x + a)(x + b) \text{ or}$$
$$(ac)x^2 + (ad + bc)x + bd = (ax + b)(cx + d).$$

For factors with four terms, look for groups to factor. Once you have found the factors, write the original polynomial as the product of all the factors. Make sure all of the polynomial factors are prime. Monomial factors may be prime or composite. Check your work by multiplying the factors to make sure you get the original polynomial.

Equation: States that two mathematical expressions are equal.

One Variable Linear Equation: An equation written in the form $ax + b = 0$, where $a \neq 0$.

Root: A solution to a one-variable equation; a number that makes the equation true when it is substituted for the variable.

Solution Set: The set of all solutions of an equation.

Empty Set: A situation in which an equation has no true solution.

Equivalent Equations: Equations with identical solution sets.

Complex Fraction: A fraction that contains a fraction in its numerator, denominator, or both. These can be solved in a number of ways, with the simplest being by following the order of operations.

For example, $\dfrac{\left(\frac{4}{7}\right)}{\left(\frac{5}{8}\right)} = \dfrac{0.571}{0.625} = 0.914.$

Another way to solve this problem is to multiply the fraction in the numerator by the reciprical of the fraction in the denominator

For example, $\dfrac{\left(\frac{4}{7}\right)}{\left(\frac{5}{8}\right)} = \dfrac{4}{7} \times \dfrac{8}{5} = \dfrac{32}{35} = 0.914.$

Absolute Value: The distance a number is from zero; always a positive number or zero. The absolute value of a number, x, is written $|x|$.

Multiply all terms by the lowest common denominator to eliminate any fractions. Look for addition or subtraction to undo so you can isolate the variable on one side of the equal sign. Divide both sides by the coefficient of the variable. When you have a value for the variable, substitute this value into the original equation to make sure you have a true equation.

Explain *inequalities*, including *conditional inequalities* and *absolute inequalities*.

Discuss one-variable quadratic equations.

Explain how to solve quadratic equations by factoring.

Explain how to complete the square to solve a quadratic equation.

Discuss the *quadratic formula*.

Explain how *simple* and *compound interest* are calculated.

One-Variable Quadratic Equation: An equation that can be written in the form $x^2 + bx + c = 0$, where a, b, and c are the coefficients. This is also known as the standard form of an equation.

The solutions of quadratic equations are called roots. A quadratic equation may have one real root, two different real roots, or no real roots. The roots can be found using one of three methods: factoring, completing the square, or using the quadratic formula.

Any time you are solving a quadratic equation, never divide both sides by the variable or any expression containing the variable. You are at risk of dividing by zero if you do, thus getting an extraneous, or invalid, root.

Inequality: A mathematical statement showing that two mathematical expressions are not equal. Inequalities use the > (greater than) and < (less than) symbols rather than the equal sign. Graphs of the solution set of inequalities are represented on a number line. Open circles are used to show that an equation approaches a number but is never equal to that number.

Conditional inequality: An inequality that has certain values for the variable that will make the condition true, and other values for the variable that will make the condition false.

Absolute inequality: An inequality that can have any real number as the value for the variable to make the condition true, and no real number value for the variable that will make the condition false.

To solve an inequality, follow the same rules as solving an equation. However, when multiplying or dividing an inequality by a negative number, you must reverse the direction of the inequality sign.

Double Inequality: A situation in which two inequality statements apply to the same variable expression.

When working with absolute values in inequalities, apply the following rules:

$$|ax + b| < c \Rightarrow -c < ax + b < c$$
$$|ax + b| > c \Rightarrow ax + b < -c \text{ or } ax + b > c$$

To complete the square, rewrite the equation so that all terms containing the variable are on the left side of the equal sign, and all the constants are on the right side of the equal sign. Make sure the coefficient of the squared term is 1. If there is a coefficient with the squared term, divide each term on both sides of the equal side by that number. Next, work with the coefficient of the single-variable term. Square half of this coefficient, and add that value to both sides. Now you can factor the left side (the side containing the variable) as the square of a binomial. $x^2 + 2ax + a^2 = C \Rightarrow (x + a)^2 = C$, where x is the variable, and a and C are constants. Take the square root of both sides and solve for the variable. Substitute the value of the variable in the original problem to check your work.

Begin by rewriting the equation in standard form, if necessary. Factor the side with the variable. Set each of the factors equal to zero and solve the resulting linear equations. Check your answers by substituting the roots you found into the original equation.

If, when writing the equation in standard form, you have an equation in the form $x^2 + c = 0$ or $x^2 - c = 0$, set $x^2 = -c$ or $x^2 = c$ and take the square root of c. If $c = 0$, the only real root is zero. If c is positive, there are two real roots—the positive and negative square root values. If c is negative, there are no real roots because you cannot take the square root of a negative number.

Simple Interest: Interest that is paid once per year for the principal amount. The formula is $I = Prt$, where I is the amount of interest, P is the principal, or original amount, r is the annual interest rate, and t is the amount of time, in years.

Compound Interest: Interest that is paid multiple times per year for the amount of the principal plus accrued interest. The formula is

$P = P_0 \left(1 + \frac{r}{n}\right)^{nt}$, where P is the total value of the investment, P_0 is the initial value, t is the amount of time in years, r is the annual interest rate, and n is the number of times per year the interest is compounded.

The quadratic formula is used to solve quadratic equations when other methods are more difficult. To use the quadratic formula to solve a quadratic equation, begin by rewriting the equation in standard form $ax^2 + bx + c = 0$, where a, b, and c are coefficients. Once you have identified the values of the coefficients, substitute those values into the quadratic formula $x = \frac{-b \pm \sqrt{b^2 - 4ac}}{2a}$. Evaluate the equation and simplify the expression. Again, check each root by substituting into the original equation.

In the quadratic formula, the portion of the formula under the radical $(b^2 - 4ac)$ is called the discriminant. If the discriminant is zero, there is only one root: zero. If the discriminant is positive, there are two different real roots. If the discriminant is negative, there are no real roots.

Explain the relationship between *distance*, *rate*, and *time*.

Explain how to solve radical equations.

Define the following common arithmetic terms specific to numbers: integers, prime, composite, even, and odd.

Describe rational, irrational, and real numbers.

Define the term factor, and explain common and prime factors with examples.

Explain fractions, numerators, and denominators.

Begin by isolating the radical term on one side of the equation, and move all other terms to the other side of the equation. Look at the index of the radicand. Remember, if no number is given, the index is 2, meaning square root. Raise both sides of the equation to the power equal to the index of the radical. Solve the resulting equation as you would a normal polynomial equation. When you have found the roots, you MUST check them in the original problem to ensure that they are all valid roots.

Distance is achieved by moving at a given rate for a given length of time. The formulas that relate the three are

$$d = rt, \ r = \frac{d}{t}, \text{ and } t = \frac{d}{r},$$ where d is the distance, r is the rate of change over time, and t is total time. In these formulas, the units used to express the rate must be the same units used to express the distance and the time.

Rational, irrational, and real numbers can be described as follows: Rational numbers include all integers, decimals, and fractions. Any terminating or repeating decimal number is a rational number. Irrational numbers cannot be written as fractions or decimals because the number of decimal places is infinite and there is no recurring pattern of digits within the number. For example, pi (π) begins with 3.141592 and continues without terminating or repeating, so pi is an irrational number.
Real numbers are the set of all rational and irrational numbers.

Numbers are the basic building blocks of mathematics. Specific features of numbers are identified by the following terms:
Integers – The set of positive and negative numbers, including zero. Integers do not include fractions ($\frac{1}{3}$), decimals (0.56), or mixed numbers ($7\frac{3}{4}$).
Prime number – A whole number greater than 1 that has only two factors, itself and 1; that is, a number that can be divided evenly only by 1 and itself.
Composite number – A whole number greater than 1 that has more than two different factors; in other words, any whole number that is not a prime number. For example: The composite number 8 has the factors of 1, 2, 4, and 8.
Even number – Any integer that can be divided by 2 without leaving a remainder. For example: 2, 4, 6, 8, and so on.
Odd number – Any integer that cannot be divided evenly by 2. For example: 3, 5, 7, 9, and so on.

A fraction is a number that is expressed as one integer written above another integer, with a dividing line between them ($\frac{x}{y}$). It represents the quotient of the two numbers "x divided by y." It can also be thought of as x out of y equal parts.
The top number of a fraction is called the numerator, and it represents the number of parts under consideration. The 1 in $\frac{1}{4}$ means that 1 part out of the whole is being considered in the calculation. The bottom number of a fraction is called the denominator, and it represents the total number of equal parts. The 4 in $\frac{1}{4}$ means that the whole consists of 4 equal parts.
A fraction cannot have a denominator of zero; this is referred to as "undefined."

Factors are numbers that are multiplied together to obtain a product. For example, in the equation 2 × 3 = 6, the numbers 2 and 3 are factors. A prime number has only two factors (1 and itself), but other numbers can have many factors.
A common factor is a number that divides exactly into two or more other numbers. For example, the factors of 12 are 1, 2, 3, 4, 6, and 12, while the factors of 15 are 1, 3, 5, and 15. The common factors of 12 and 15 are 1 and 3.
A prime factor is also a prime number. Therefore, the prime factors of 12 are 1, 2, and 3. For 15, the prime factors are 1, 3, and 5.

Explain the decimal system and define the terms decimal, decimal point, and decimal place.

List the four basic mathematical operations and give examples of each.

Explain the correct Order of Operations, including a discussion of PEMDAS.

Define greatest common factor (GCF) and least common multiple (LCM).

Describe how to manipulating fractions, including how to simplify a fraction and find a common denominator.

Explain the relationships between percentages, fractions, and decimals.

There are four basic mathematical operations:

Addition increases the value of one quantity by the value of another quantity. Example: 2 + 4 = 6; 8 + 9 = 17. The result is called the sum. With addition, the order does not matter. 4 + 2 = 2 + 4.

Subtraction is the opposite operation to addition; it decreases the value of one quantity by the value of another quantity. Example: 6 – 4 = 2; 17 – 8 = 9. The result is called the difference. Note that with subtraction, the order does matter. 6 – 4 ≠ 4 – 6.

Multiplication can be thought of as repeated addition. One number tells how many times to add the other number to itself. Example: 3 × 2 (three times two) = 2 + 2 + 2 = 6. With multiplication, the order does not matter. 2 × 3 (or 3 + 3) = 3 × 2 (or 2 + 2 + 2).

Division is the opposite operation to multiplication; one number tells us how many parts to divide the other number into. Example: 20 ÷ 4 = 5; if 20 is split into 4 equal parts, each part is 5. With division, the order of the numbers does matter. 20 ÷ 4 ≠ 4 ÷ 20.

The decimal, or base 10, system is a number system that uses ten different digits (0, 1, 2, 3, 4, 5, 6, 7, 8, 9). An example of a number system that uses something other than ten digits is the binary, or base 2, number system, used by computers, which uses only the numbers 0 and 1. It is thought that the decimal system originated because people had only their 10 fingers for counting.

Decimal – a number that uses a decimal point to show the part of the number that is less than one. Example: 1.234.

Decimal point – a symbol used to separate the ones place from the tenths place in decimals or dollars from cents in currency.

Decimal place – the position of a number to the right of the decimal point. In the decimal 0.123, the 1 is in the first place to the right of the decimal point, indicating tenths; the 2 is in the second place, indicating hundredths; and the 3 is in the third place, indicating thousandths.

The greatest common factor (GCF) is the largest number that is a factor of two or more numbers. For example, the factors of 15 are 1, 3, 5, and 15; the factors of 35 are 1, 5, 7, and 35. Therefore, the greatest common factor of 15 and 35 is 5.

The least common multiple (LCM) is the smallest number that is a multiple of two or more numbers. For example, the multiples of 3 include 3, 6, 9, 12, 15, etc.; the multiples of 5 include 5, 10, 15, 20, etc. Therefore, the least common multiple of 3 and 5 is 15.

Order of Operations is a set of rules that dictates the order in which we must perform each operation in an expression so that we will evaluate at accurately. If we have an expression that includes multiple different operations, Order of Operations tells us which operations to do first. The most common mnemonic for Order of Operations is PEMDAS, or "Please Excuse My Dear Aunt Sally." PEMDAS stands for Parentheses, Exponents, Multiplication, Division, Addition, Subtraction. It is important to understand that multiplication and division have equal precedence, as do addition and subtraction, so those pairs of operations are simply worked from left to right in order.

Example: Evaluate the expression $5 + 20 \div 4 \times (2 + 3)^2 - 6$ using the correct order of operations.

P: Perform the operations inside the parentheses, (2 + 3) = 5.

E: Simplify the exponents, $(5)^2 = 25$.

The equation now looks like this: 5 + 20 ÷ 4 × 25 – 6.

MD: Perform multiplication and division from left to right, 20 ÷ 4 = 5; then 5 × 25 = 125.

The equation now looks like this: 5 + 125 – 6.

AS: Perform addition and subtraction from left to right, 5 + 125 = 130; then 130 – 6 = 124.

Percentages can be thought of as fractions that are based on a whole of 100; that is, one whole is equal to 100%. The word percent means "per hundred." Fractions can be expressed as percents by finding equivalent fractions with a denomination of 100. Example: $\frac{7}{10} = \frac{70}{100} = 70\%$; $\frac{1}{4} = \frac{25}{100} = 25\%$.

To express a percentage as a fraction, divide the percentage number by 100 and reduce the fraction to its simplest possible terms. Example: $60\% = \frac{60}{100} = \frac{3}{5}$; $96\% = \frac{96}{100} = \frac{24}{25}$.

Converting decimals to percentages and percentages to decimals is as simple as moving the decimal point. To convert from a decimal to a percent, move the decimal point two places to the right. To convert from a percent to a decimal, move it two places to the left. Example: 0.23 = 23%; 5.34 = 534%; 0.007 = 0.7%; 700% = 7.00; 86% = 0.86; 0.15% = 0.0015.

It may be helpful to remember that the percentage number will always be larger than the equivalent decimal number.

Fractions can be manipulated by multiplying or dividing (but not adding or subtracting) both the numerator and denominator by the same number, without changing the value of the fraction. If you divide both numbers by a common factor, you are reducing or simplifying the fraction. Two fractions that have the same value, but are expressed differently are known as equivalent fractions. For example, $\frac{2}{10}, \frac{3}{15}, \frac{4}{20}$, and $\frac{5}{25}$ are all equivalent fractions. They can also all be reduced or simplified to $\frac{1}{5}$.

When two fractions are manipulated so that they have the same denominator, this is known as finding a common denominator. The number chosen to be that common denominator should be the least common multiple of the two original denominators. Example: $\frac{3}{4}$ and $\frac{5}{6}$; the least common multiple of 4 and 6 is 12. Manipulating to achieve the common denominator: $\frac{3}{4} = \frac{9}{12}$; $\frac{5}{6} = \frac{10}{12}$.

Discuss percentage problems and the process to be used for solving them.

Discuss improper fractions and mixed numbers.

Describe the process for adding, subtracting, multiplying, and dividing fractions.

Describe exponents and parentheses.

List the laws of exponents.

Discuss roots and explain how they relate to exponents.

A fraction whose denominator is greater than its numerator is known as a proper fraction, while a fraction whose numerator is greater than its denominator is known as an improper fraction. Proper fractions have values less than one and improper fractions have values greater than one.

A mixed number is a number that contains both an integer and a fraction. Any improper fraction can be rewritten as a mixed number. Example: $\frac{8}{3} = \frac{6}{3} + \frac{2}{3} = 2 + \frac{2}{3} = 2\frac{2}{3}$. Similarly, any mixed number can be rewritten as an improper fraction. Example: $1\frac{3}{5} = 1 + \frac{3}{5} = \frac{5}{5} + \frac{3}{5} = \frac{8}{5}$.

A percentage problem can be presented three main ways:
(1) Find what percentage of some number another number is. Example: What percentage of 40 is 8?
(2) Find what number is some percentage of a given number. Example: What number is 20% of 40?
(3) Find what number another number is a given percentage of. Example: What number is 8 20% of?
The three components in all of these cases are the same: a whole (W), a part (P), and a percentage (%). These are related by the equation: $P = W \times \%$. This is the form of the equation you would use to solve problems of type (2). To solve types (1) and (3), you would use these two forms: $\% = P/W$ and $W = P/\%$.
The thing that frequently makes percentage problems difficult is that they are often also word problems, so a large part of solving them is figuring out which quantities are what. Example: In a school cafeteria, 7 students choose pizza, 9 choose hamburgers, and 4 choose tacos. Find the percentage that chooses tacos. To find the whole, you must first add all of the parts: $7 + 9 + 4 = 20$. The percentage can then be found by dividing the part by the whole ($\% = P/W$): $\frac{4}{20} = \frac{20}{100} = 20\%$

An exponent is a superscript number placed next to another number at the top right. It indicates how many times the base number is to be multiplied by itself. Exponents provide a shorthand way to write what would be a longer mathematical expression. Example: $a^2 = a \times a$; $2^4 = 2 \times 2 \times 2 \times 2$. A number with an exponent of 2 is said to be "squared," while a number with an exponent of 3 is said to be "cubed." The value of a number raised to an exponent is called its power. So, 8^4 is read as "8 to the 4th power," or "8 raised to the power of 4." A negative exponent is the same as the reciprocal of a positive exponent. Example: $a^{-2} = 1/a^2$. Parentheses are used to designate which operations should be done first when there are multiple operations. Example: $4 - (2 + 1) = 1$; the parentheses tell us that we must add 2 and 1, and then subtract the sum from 4, rather than subtracting 2 from 4 and then adding 1 (this would give us an answer of 3).

If two fractions have a common denominator, they can be added or subtracted simply by adding or subtracting the two numerators and retaining the same denominator. Example: $\frac{1}{2} + \frac{1}{4} = \frac{2}{4} + \frac{1}{4} = \frac{3}{4}$. If the two fractions do not already have the same denominator, one or both of them must be manipulated to achieve a common denominator before they can be added or subtracted.
Two fractions can be multiplied by multiplying the two numerators to find the new numerator and the two denominators to find the new denominator. Example: $\frac{1}{3} \times \frac{2}{3} = \frac{1 \times 2}{3 \times 3} = \frac{2}{9}$.
Two fractions can be divided flipping the numerator and denominator of the second fraction and then proceeding as though it were a multiplication. Example: $\frac{2}{3} \div \frac{3}{4} = \frac{2}{3} \times \frac{4}{3} = \frac{8}{9}$.

A root, such as a square root, is another way of writing a fractional exponent. Instead of using a superscript, roots use the radical symbol ($\sqrt{}$) to indicate the operation. A radical will have a number underneath the bar, and may sometimes have a number in the upper left: $\sqrt[n]{a}$, read as "the nth root of a." The relationship between radical notation and exponent notation can be described by this equation: $\sqrt[n]{a} = a^{1/n}$. The two special cases of $n = 2$ and $n = 3$ are called square roots and cube roots. If there is no number to the upper left, it is understood to be a square root ($n = 2$). Nearly all of the roots you encounter will be square roots. A square root is the same as a number raised to the one-half power. When we say that a is the square root of b ($a = \sqrt{b}$), we mean that a multiplied by itself equals b: ($a \times a = b$).
A perfect square is a number that has an integer for its square root. There are 10 perfect squares from 1 to 100: 1, 4, 9, 16, 25, 36, 49, 64, 81, 100 (the squares of integers 1 through 10).

The laws of exponents are as follows:
1) Any number to the power of 1 is equal to itself: $a^1 = a$.
2) The number 1 raised to any power is equal to 1: $1^n = 1$.
3) Any number raised to the power of 0 is equal to 1: $a^0 = 1$.
4) Add exponents to multiply powers of the same base number: $a^n \times a^m = a^{n+m}$.
5) Subtract exponents to divide powers of the same number: $a^n \div a^m = a^{n-m}$.
6) Multiply exponents to raise a power to a power: $(a^n)^m = a^{n \times m}$.
7) If multiplied or divided numbers inside parentheses are collectively raised to a power, this is the same as each individual term being raised to that power: $(a \times b)^n = a^n \times b^n$; $(a \div b)^n = a^n \div b^n$.

Note: Exponents do not have to be integers. Fractional or decimal exponents follow all the rules above as well. Example: $5^{\frac{1}{4}} \times 5^{\frac{3}{4}} = 5^{\frac{1}{4}+\frac{3}{4}} = 5^1 = 5$.

Explain scientific notation.

Define ratio and proportion and give examples.

Discuss some common conversions for length in the U.S. Customary System

Discuss some common prefixes used in the metric system.

Discuss the standard units in the metric system compared to the U.S. Customary System.

Discuss some common conversions for liquid capacity in the U.S. Customary System.

A ratio is a comparison of two quantities in a particular order. Example: if there are 14 computers in a lab, and the class has 20 students, there is a student to computer ratio of 20 to 14, commonly written as 20:14.

A proportion is a relationship between two quantities that dictates how one changes when the other changes. A direct proportion describes a relationship in which a quantity increases by a set amount for every increase in the other quantity, or decreases by that same amount for every decrease in the other quantity. Example: For every 1 sheet cake, 18 people can be served cake. The number of sheet cakes, and the number of people that can be served from them is directly proportional. Inverse proportion is a relationship in which an increase in one quantity is accompanied by a decrease in the other, or vice versa. Example: the time required for a car trip decreases as the speed increases, and increases as the speed decreases, so the time required is inversely proportional to the speed of the car.

Scientific notation is a way of writing large numbers in a shorter form. The form $a \times 10^n$ is used in scientific notation, where a is greater than or equal to 1, but less than 10, and n is the number of places the decimal must move to get from the original number to a.

Example: The number 230,400,000 is cumbersome to write. To write the value in scientific notation, place a decimal point between the first and second numbers, and include all digits through the last non-zero digit (a = 2.304). To find the appropriate power of 10, count the number of places the decimal point had to move (n = 8). The number is positive if the decimal moved to the left, and negative if it moved to the right. We can then write 230,400,000 as 2.304×10^8.

If we look instead at the number 0.00002304, we have the same value for a, but this time the decimal moved 5 places to the right (n = -5). Thus, 0.00002304 can be written as 2.304×10^{-5}. Using this notation makes it simple to compare very large or very small numbers. By comparing exponents, it is easy to see that 3.28×10^4 is smaller than 1.51×10^5, because 4 is less than 5.

Milli – one one-thousandth, or .001
Centi – one one-hundredth, or .01
Kilo – one thousand, or 1,000

1 foot = 12 inches
1 yard = 3 feet
1 mile = 5,280 feet

1 cup = 8 fluid ounces
1 pint = 2 cups
1 quart = 2 pints
1 gallon = 4 quarts

Metric System
Length: meter
Mass or weight: gram
Volume: liter
Temperature: Degrees Celsius
U.S. Customary System
Length: inch, foot, yard, mile
Capacity or volume: pint, quart, gallon
Mass or weight: ounce, pound, ton
Temperature, degrees Fahrenheit

Discuss some common conversions for weight in the U.S. Customary System

Describe systems of equations.

Explain how to solve systems of two linear equations by substitution. Solve using substitution:
$$x + 6y = 15$$
$$3x - 12y = 18$$

Explain how to solve systems of two linear equations by elimination. Solve using elimination:
$$x + 6y = 15$$
$$3x - 12y = 18$$

Explain how to use the trace feature of a graphing calculator to solve systems of equations.

Explain how to graph two-variable linear inequalities.

System of Equations: A set of simultaneous equations that all use the same variables. A solution to a system of equations must be true for each equation in the system.
Consistent System: A system of equations that has at least one solution.
Inconsistent System: A system of equations that has no solution.
Systems of equations may be solved using one of four methods: substitution, elimination, transformation of the augmented matrix and using the trace feature on a graphing calculator.

1 pound = 16 ounces
1 ton = 2,000 pounds

To solve a system of equations using elimination, begin by rewriting both equations in standard form $Ax + By = C$. Check to see if the coefficients of one pair of like variables adds to zero. If not, multiply one or both of the equations by a non-zero number to make one set of like variables add to zero. Add the two equations to solve for one of the variables. Substitute back into either original equation to solve for the other variable. Check your work by substituting into the other equation.
Example: Solve the system using elimination:
$$x + 6y = 15$$
$$3x - 12y = 18$$
If we multiply the first equation by 2, we can eliminate the y terms:
$$2x + 12y = 30$$
$$3x - 12y = 18$$
Add the equations together and solve for x:
$$5x = 48$$
$$x = \frac{48}{5} = 9.6$$
Plug value for x back into either of the original equations and solve for y:
$$9.6 + 6y = 15$$
$$y = \frac{15 - 9.6}{6} = 0.9$$

To solve a system of linear equations by substitution, start with the easier equation and solve for one of the variables. Express this variable in terms of the other variable. Substitute this expression into the other equation, and solve for the other variable. The solution should be expressed in the form (x, y). Substitute the values into both of the original equations to check your answer.
Example: Solve the following system using substitution:
$$x + 6y = 15$$
$$3x - 12y = 18$$
Solve the first equation for x:
$$x = 15 - 6y$$
Substitute this value in place of x in the second equation, and solve for y:
$$3(15 - 6y) - 12y = 18$$
$$45 - 18y - 12y = 18$$
$$30y = 27$$
$$y = \frac{27}{30} = \frac{9}{10} = 0.9$$
Plug this value for y back into the first equation to solve for x:
$$x = 15 - 6(0.9) = 15 - 5.4 = 9.6$$

Whenever you have an inequality using the symbol < or >, always use a dashed line for the graph. If the inequality uses the symbol ≤ or ≥, use a solid line since equal is an option. All graphs of linear inequalities require that all the area to one side of the line be shaded. To determine which side to shade, select any point that is not on the line (the origin is an easy point to use if it is not on the line) and substitute the x- and y-values into the inequality. If the inequality is true, shade the side with that point. If the inequality is false, shade the other side of the line.

Using the trace feature on a calculator requires that you rewrite each equation, isolating the y-variable on one side of the equal sign. Enter both equations in the graphing calculator and plot the graphs simultaneously. Use the trace cursor to find where the two lines cross. Use the zoom feature if necessary to obtain more accurate results. Always check your answer by substituting into the original equations. The trace method is likely to be less accurate than other methods due to the resolution of graphing calculators, but is a useful tool to provide an approximate answer.

Describe the Cartesian coordinate plane.

Describe the equation of a line in standard form, slope-intercept form, point-slope form, two-point form, and intercept form.

Define the following terms: *slope, horizontal, vertical, parallel, perpendicular.*

Explain how to find the midpoint of two points and the distance between two points.

Explain how to find the perpendicular distance between a line and a point not on the line.

Discuss *functions*, including *domain, range, independent* and *dependent variables*, and the *vertical line test.*

Standard form: $Ax + By = C$; the slope is $\frac{-A}{B}$ and the y-intercept is $\frac{C}{B}$.

Slope-Intercept form: $y = mx + b$, where m is the slope and b is the y-intercept.

Point-Slope form: $y - y_1 = m(x - x_1)$, where m is the slope and (x_1, y_1) is a point on the line.

Two-Point form: $\frac{y - y_1}{x - x_1} = \frac{y_2 - y_1}{x_2 - x_1}$, where (x_1, y_1) and (x_2, y_2) are two points on the given line.

Intercept form: $\frac{x}{x_1} + \frac{y}{y_1} = 1$, where $(x_1, 0)$ is the point at which a line intersects the x-axis, and $(0, y_1)$ is the point at which the same line intersects the y-axis.

The Cartesian coordinate plane consists of two number lines placed perpendicular to each other, and intersecting at the zero point, also known as the origin. The horizontal number line is known as the x-axis, with positive values to the right of the origin, and negative values to the left of the origin. The vertical number line is known as the y-axis, with positive values above the origin, and negative values below the origin. Any point on the plane can be identified by an ordered pair in the form (x,y), called coordinates. The x-value of the coordinate is called the abscissa, and the y-value of the coordinate is called the ordinate. The two number lines divide the plane into four quadrants: I, II, III, and IV.

To find the midpoint of two points (x_1, y_1) and (x_2, y_2), average the x-coordinates to get the x-coordinate of the midpoint, and average the y-coordinates to get the y-coordinate of the midpoint. The formula is

$$\text{midpoint} = \left(\frac{x_1 + x_2}{2}, \frac{y_1 + y_2}{2}\right)$$

The distance between two points is the same as the length of the hypotenuse of a right triangle with the two given points as endpoints, and the two sides of the right triangle parallel to the x-axis and y-axis, respectively. The length of the segment parallel to the x-axis is the difference between the x-coordinates of the two points. The length of the segment parallel to the y-axis is the difference between the y-coordinates of the two points. Use the Pythagorean Theorem $a^2 + b^2 = c^2$ or $c = \sqrt{a^2 + b^2}$ to find the distance. The formula is:

$$\text{distance} = \sqrt{(x_2 - x_1)^2 + (y_2 - y_1)^2}$$

Slope: A ratio of the change in height to the change in horizontal distance. On a graph with two points (x_1, y_1) and (x_2, y_2), the slope is represented by the formula $m = \frac{y_2 - y_1}{x_2 - x_1}$; $x_1 \neq x_2$. If the value of the slope is positive, the line slopes upward from left to right. If the value of the slope is negative, the line slopes downward from left to right. If the y-coordinates are the same for both points, the slope is 0 and the line is a horizontal line. If the x-coordinates are the same for both points, there is no slope and the line is a vertical line.

Horizontal: Having a slope of zero. On a graph, a line that is the same distance from the x-axis at all points.

Vertical: Having no slope. On a graph, a line that is the same distance from the y-axis at all points.

Parallel: Lines that have equal slopes.

Perpendicular: Lines that have slopes that are negative reciprocals of each other:

$\frac{a}{b}$ and $\frac{-b}{a}$.

A function is an equation that has exactly one value of output variable (dependent variable) for each value of the input variable (independent variable). The set of all values for the input variable (here assumed to be x) is the domain of the function, and the set of all corresponding values of output variable (here assumed to be y) is the range of the function. When looking at a graph of an equation, the easiest way to determine if the equation is a function or not is to conduct the vertical line test. If a vertical line drawn through any value of x crosses the graph in more than one place, the equation is not a function.

If the equation for the line is not given to you in the format $Ax + By + C = 0$, you will need to convert it to this format. Once you have it in that format, you can use the formula:

$$d = \frac{|Ax_1 + By_1 + C|}{\sqrt{A^2 + B^2}}$$

where (x_1, y_1) are the coordinates of the point in question.

Discuss the following properties of functions: *argument*, *domain of definition*, *graph*, *zeros*, *roots*, and *intercepts*.

Explain *horizontal shift* and *vertical shift* as they apply to the graphs of functions.

Explain *stretch*, *compression*, and *reflection* as they relate to the graphs of functions.

Explain *exponential functions* and *logarithmic functions* and the relationship between the two.

Discuss *linear functions.*

Discuss *constant functions* and, *identity functions.*

Horizontal and vertical shift occur when values are added to or subtracted from the x or y values, respectively.

If a constant is added to the y portion of each point, the graph shifts up. If a constant is subtracted from the y portion of each point, the graph shifts down. This is represented by the expression $f(x) \pm k$, where k is a constant.

If a constant is added to the x portion of each point, the graph shifts left. If a constant is subtracted from the x portion of each point, the graph shifts right. This is represented by the expression $f(x \pm k)$, where k is a constant.

In functions with the notation $f(x)$, the value substituted for x in the equation is called the argument. The domain is the set of all values for x in a function. Unless otherwise given, assume the domain is the set of real numbers that will yield real numbers for the range. This is the domain of definition.

The graph of a function is the set of all ordered pairs (x, y) that satisfy the equation of the function. The points that have zero as the value for y are called the zeros of the function. These are also the x-intercepts, because that is the point at which the graph crosses, or intercepts, the x-axis. The points that have zero as the value for x are the y-intercepts because that is where the graph crosses the y-axis.

Exponential functions are equations that have the format $y = b^x$, where base $b > 0$ and $b \neq 1$. The exponential function can also be written $f(x) = b^x$. **Logarithmic functions** are equations that have the format $y = \log_b x$ or $f(x) = \log_b x$. The base b may be any number except one; however, the most common bases for logarithms are base 10 and base e. The log base e is known the natural logarithm, or ln, expressed by the function $f(x) = \ln x$. Any logarithm that does not have an assigned value of b is assumed to be base 10: $\log x = \log_{10} x$. Exponential functions and logarithmic functions are related in that one is the inverse of the other. If $f(x) = b^x$, then $f^{-1}(x) = \log_b x$. This can perhaps be expressed more clearly by the two equations: $y = b^x$ and $x = \log_b y$. The following properties apply to logarithmic expressions:

$$\log_b 1 = 0$$
$$\log_b b = 1$$
$$\log_b b^p = p$$
$$\log_b MN = \log_b M + \log_b N$$
$$\log_b \frac{M}{N} = \log_b M - \log_b N$$
$$\log_b M^p = p \log_b M$$

Stretch, compression, and reflection occur when different parts of a function are multiplied by different groups of constants. If the function as a whole is multiplied by a real number constant greater than 1 $(k \times f(x))$, the graph is stretched vertically. If k in the previous equation is greater than zero but less than 1, the graph is compressed vertically. If k is less than zero, the graph is reflected about the x-axis, in addition to being either stretched or compressed vertically if k is less than or greater than -1, respectively.

If instead, just the x-term is multiplied by a constant greater than 1 $(f(k \times x))$, the graph is compressed horizontally. If k in the previous equation is greater than zero but less than 1, the graph is stretched horizontally. If k is less than zero, the graph is reflected about the y-axis, in addition to being either stretched or compressed horizontally if k is greater than or less than -1, respectively.

Constant functions are given by the equation $y = b$ or $f(x) = b$, where b is a real number. There is no independent variable present in the equation, so the function has a constant value for all x. The graph of a constant function is a horizontal line of slope 0 that is positioned b units from the x-axis. If b is positive, the line is above the x-axis; if b is negative, the line is below the x-axis.

Identity functions are identified by the equation $y = x$ or $f(x) = x$, where every value of y is equal to its corresponding value of x. The only zero is the point $(0, 0)$. The graph is a diagonal line with slope 1.

In **linear functions**, the value of the function changes in direct proportion to x. The rate of change, represented by the slope on its graph, is constant throughout. The standard form of a linear equation is $ax + by = c$, where a, b, and c are real numbers. As a function, this equation is commonly written as $y = mx + b$ or $f(x) = mx + b$. This is known as the slope-intercept form, because the coefficients give the slope of the graphed function (m) and its y-intercept (b). Solve the equation $mx + b = 0$ for x to get $= -\frac{b}{m}$, which is the only zero of the function. The domain and range are both the set of all real numbers.

Discuss the characteristics of a *quadratic function*.

Describe the graphs of quadratic functions.

Discuss the *Fundamental Theorem of Algebra*, the *Remainder Theorem*, and the *Factor Theorem* as they apply to functions.

Discuss the *Rational Root Theorem* as it applies to functions.

Discuss *rational functions*.

Discuss *square root functions*.

A quadratic function has a parabola for its graph. In the equation $f(x) = ax^2 + bx + c$, if a is positive, the parabola will open upward. If a is negative, the parabola will open downward. The axis of symmetry is a vertical line that passes through the vertex. To determine whether or not the parabola will intersect the x-axis, check the number of real roots. An equation with two real roots will cross the x-axis twice. An equation with one real root will have its vertex on the x-axis. An equation with no real roots will not contact the x-axis.

A **quadratic function** is a polynomial function that follows the equation pattern $y = ax^2 + bx + c$, or $f(x) = ax^2 + bx + c$, where a, b, and c are real numbers and $a \neq 0$. The domain of a quadratic function is the set of all real numbers. The range is also real numbers, but only those in the subset of the domain that satisfy the equation. The root(s) of any quadratic function can be found by plugging the values of a, b, and c into the **quadratic formula**:

$$x = \frac{-b \pm \sqrt{b^2 - 4ac}}{2a}$$

If the expression $b^2 - 4ac$ is negative, you will instead find complex roots.

According to the **Rational Root Theorem,** any rational root of a polynomial function $f(x) = a_n x^n + a_{n-1} x^{n-1} + \cdots + a_1 x + a_0$ with integer coefficients will, when reduced to its lowest terms, be a positive or negative fraction such that the numerator is a factor of a_0 and the denominator is a factor of a_n. For instance, if the polynomial function $f(x) = x^3 + 3x^2 - 4$ has any rational roots, the numerators of those roots can only be factors of 4 (1, 2, 4), and the denominators can only be factors of 1 (1). The function in this example has roots of 1 (or $\frac{1}{1}$) and -2 (or $-\frac{2}{1}$).

According to the **Fundamental Theorem of Algebra**, every non-constant, single variable polynomial has exactly as many roots as the polynomial's highest exponent. For example, if x^4 is the largest exponent of a term, the polynomial will have exactly 4 roots. However, some of these roots may have multiplicity or be non-real numbers. For instance, in the polynomial function $f(x) = x^4 - 4x + 3$, the only real roots are 1 and -1. The root 1 has multiplicity of 2 and there is one non-real root $(-1 - \sqrt{2}i)$.

The **Remainder Theorem** is useful for determining the remainder when a polynomial is divided by a binomial. The Remainder Theorem states that if a polynomial function $f(x)$ is divided by a binomial $x - a$, where a is a real number, the remainder of the division will be the value of $f(a)$. If $f(a) = 0$, then a is a root of the polynomial.

The **Factor Theorem** is related to the Remainder Theorem and states that if $f(a) = 0$ then $(x - a)$ is a factor of the function.

A **square root function** is a function that contains a radical and is in the format $f(x) = \sqrt{ax + b}$. The domain is the set of all real numbers that yields a positive radicand or a radicand equal to zero. Because square root values are assumed to be positive unless otherwise identified, the range is all real numbers from zero to infinity. To find the zero of a square root function, set the radicand equal to zero and solve for x. The graph of a square root function is always to the right of the zero and always above the x-axis.

A **rational function** is a function that can be constructed as a ratio of two polynomial expressions: $f(x) = \frac{p(x)}{q(x)}$, where $p(x)$ and $q(x)$ are both polynomial expressions and $q(x) \neq 0$. The domain is the set of all real numbers, except any values for which $q(x) = 0$. The range is the set of real numbers that satisfies the function when the domain is applied. When you graph a rational function, you will have vertical asymptotes wherever $q(x) = 0$. If the polynomial in the numerator is of lesser degree than the polynomial in the denominator, the x-axis will also be a horizontal asymptote. If the numerator and denominator have equal degrees, there will be a horizontal asymptote not on the x-axis. If the degree of the numerator is exactly one greater than the degree of the denominator, the graph will have an oblique, or diagonal, asymptote. The asymptote will be along the line $y = \frac{p_n}{q_{n-1}} x + \frac{p_{n-1}}{q_{n-1}}$, where p_n and q_{n-1} are the coefficients of the highest degree terms in their respective polynomials.

Discuss *absolute value functions.*

Discuss the characteristics of *polynomial functions.*

Explain one-to-one functions and the purpose of the horizontal line test.

Explain *monotone*, *even*, and *odd* functions, and *discontinuities* in functions.

Explain the difference between variables that vary *directly* and those that vary *inversely*.

Describe the differences between *algebraic functions* and *transcendental functions.*

A **polynomial function** is a function with multiple terms and multiple powers of x, such as

$$f(x) = a_n x^n + a_{n-1} x^{n-1} + a_{n-2} x^{n-2} + \cdots + a_1 x + a_0$$

where n is a non-negative integer that is the highest exponent in the polynomial, and $a_n \neq 0$. The domain of a polynomial function is the set of all real numbers. If the greatest exponent in the polynomial is even, the polynomial is said to be of even degree and the range is the set of real numbers that satisfy the function. If the greatest exponent in the polynomial is odd, the polynomial is said to be odd and the range, like the domain, is the set of all real numbers.

An **absolute value function** is in the format $f(x) = |ax + b|$. Like other functions, the domain is the set of all real numbers. However, because absolute value indicates positive numbers, the range is limited to positive real numbers. To find the zero of an absolute value function, set the portion inside the absolute value sign equal to zero and solve for x. An absolute value function is also known as a piecewise function because it must be solved in pieces – one for if the value inside the absolute value sign is positive, and one for if the value is negative. The function can be expressed as

$$f(x) = \begin{cases} ax + b & \text{if } ax + b \geq 0 \\ -(ax + b) & \text{if } ax + b < 0 \end{cases}$$

This will allow for an accurate statement of the range.

A **monotone function** is a function whose graph either constantly increases or constantly decreases. Examples include the functions $f(x) = x$, $f(x) = -x$, or $f(x) = x^3$.

An **even function** has a graph that is symmetric with respect to the y-axis and satisfies the equation $f(x) = f(-x)$. Examples include the functions $f(x) = x^2$ and $f(x) = ax^n$, where a is any real number and n is a positive even integer.

An **odd function** has a graph that is symmetric with respect to the origin and satisfies the equation $f(x) = -f(-x)$. Examples include the functions $f(x) = x^3$ and $f(x) = ax^n$, where a is any real number and n is a positive odd integer.

Any time there are vertical asymptotes or holes in a graph, such that the complete graph cannot be drawn as one continuous line, a graph is said to have discontinuities. Examples would include the graphs of hyperbolas that are functions, and the function $f(x) = \tan x$.

In a **one-to-one function**, each value of x has exactly one value for y (this is the definition of a function) *and* each value of y has exactly one value for x. While the vertical line test will determine if a graph is that of a function, the horizontal line test will determine if a function is a one-to-one function. If a horizontal line drawn at any value of y intersects the graph in more than one place, the graph is not that of a one-to-one function. Do not make the mistake of using the horizontal line test exclusively in determining if a graph is that of a one-to-one function. A one-to-one function must pass both the vertical line test and the horizontal line test. One-to-one functions are also **invertible functions**.

Algebraic functions are those that exclusively use polynomials and roots. These would include polynomial functions, rational functions, square root functions, and all combinations of these functions, such as polynomials as the radicand. These combinations may be joined by addition, subtraction, multiplication, or division, but may not include variables as exponents.

Transcendental functions are all functions that are non-algebraic. Any function that includes logarithms, trigonometric functions, variables as exponents, or any combination that includes any of these is not algebraic in nature, even if the function includes polynomials or roots.

Variables that vary directly are those that either both increase at the same rate or both decrease at the same rate. For example, in the functions $f(x) = kx$ or $f(x) = kx^n$, where k and n are positive, the value of $f(x)$ increases as the value of x increases and decreases as the value of x decreases.

Variables that vary inversely are those where one increases while the other decreases. For example, in the functions $f(x) = \frac{k}{x}$ or $f(x) = \frac{k}{x^n}$ where k is a positive constant, the value of y increases as the value of x decreases, and the value of y decreases as the value of x increases. In both cases, k is the constant of variation.

Explain how to find the sum, difference, product, or quotient of two functions.

Explain how to find the *composite* of two functions.

Discuss the terms *limit*, *converge*, and *diverge* as they relate to sequences.

Give the properties of the sum, difference, product, quotient, and scalar multiplication of the limits of sequences.

Define *monotonic*, *nonincreasing*, and *nondecreasing* as they apply to sequences.

Describe an *infinite series*, including the *sequence of partial sums*.

The composite of two functions f and g, written as $(f \circ g)(x)$ simply means that the output of the second function is used as the input of the first. This can also be written as $f(g(x))$. In general, this can be solved by substituting $g(x)$ for all instances of x in $f(x)$ and simplifying. Using the example functions $f(x) = x^2 - x + 2$ and $g(x) = x + 1$, we can find that $(f \circ g)(x)$ or $f(g(x))$ is equal to $f(x + 1) = (x + 1)^2 - (x + 1) + 2$, which simplifies to $x^2 + x + 2$.

It is important to note that $(f \circ g)(x)$ is not necessarily the same as $(g \circ f)(x)$. The process is not commutative like addition or multiplication expressions. If $(f \circ g)(x)$ does equal $(g \circ f)(x)$, the two functions are inverses of each other.

For each operation, we will use these functions as examples: $f(x) = x^2$ and $g(x) = x$.

To find the sum of two functions f and g, assuming the domains are compatible, simply add the two functions together: $(f + g)(x) = f(x) + g(x) = x^2 + x$.

To find the difference of two functions f and g, assuming the domains are compatible, simply subtract the second function from the first: $(f - g)(x) = f(x) - g(x) = x^2 - x$.

To find the product of two functions f and g, assuming the domains are compatible, multiply the two functions together: $(f \cdot g)(x) = f(x) \cdot g(x) = x^2 \cdot x = x^3$.

To find the quotient of two functions f and g, assuming the domains are compatible, divide the first function by the second: $\frac{f}{g}(x) = \frac{f(x)}{g(x)} = \frac{x^2}{x} = x \, ; x \neq 0$.

The limit of the sums of two sequences is equal to the sum of the limits of the two sequences: $\lim_{n \to \infty}(a_n + b_n) = \lim_{n \to \infty} a_n + \lim_{n \to \infty} b_n$.
The limit of the difference between two sequences is equal to the difference between the limits of the two sequences: $\lim_{n \to \infty}(a_n - b_n) = \lim_{n \to \infty} a_n - \lim_{n \to \infty} b_n$.
The limit of the product of two sequences is equal to the product of the limits of the two sequences: $\lim_{n \to \infty}(a_n \cdot b_n) = \lim_{n \to \infty} a_n \cdot \lim_{n \to \infty} b_n$.
The limit of the quotient of two sequences is equal to the quotient of the limits of the two sequences, with some exceptions: $\lim_{n \to \infty} \left(\frac{a_n}{b_n} \right) = \frac{\lim_{n \to \infty} a_n}{\lim_{n \to \infty} b_n}$. In the quotient formula, it is important to consider that $b_n \neq 0$ and $\lim_{n \to \infty} b_n \neq 0$.
The limit of a sequence multiplied by a scalar is equal to the scalar multiplied by the limit of the sequence: $\lim_{n \to \infty} k a_n = k \lim_{n \to \infty} a_n$, where k is any real number.

Some sequences will have a limit, or a value the sequence approaches or sometimes even reaches but never passes. A sequence that has a limit is known as a convergent sequence because all the values of the sequence seemingly converge at that point. Sequences that do not converge at a particular limit are divergent sequences. The easiest way to determine whether a sequence converges or diverges is to find the limit of the sequence. If the limit is a real number, the sequence is a convergent sequence. If the limit is infinity, the sequence is a divergent sequence. Remember the following rules for finding limits:
$\lim_{n \to \infty} k = k$ for all real numbers k

$$\lim_{n \to \infty} \frac{1}{n} = 0$$
$$\lim_{n \to \infty} n = \infty$$

$\lim_{n \to \infty} \frac{k}{n^p} = 0$ for all real numbers k and positive rational numbers p.

An **infinite series**, also referred to as just a series, is a series of partial sums of a defined sequence. Each infinite sequence represents an infinite series according to the equation $\sum_{n=1}^{\infty} a_n = a_1 + a_2 + a_3 + \cdots + a_n + \cdots$. This notation can be shortened to $\sum_{n=1}^{\infty} a_n$ or $\sum a_n$. Every series is a sequence of partial sums, where the first partial sum is equal to the first element of the series, the second partial sum is equal to the sum of the first two elements of the series, and the nth partial sum is equal to the sum of the first n elements of the series.

A **monotonic sequence** is a sequence that is either nonincreasing or nondecreasing. The term *nonincreasing* is used to describe a sequence whose terms either get progressively smaller in value or remain the same. The term *nondecreasing* is used to describe a sequence whose terms either get progressively larger in value or remain the same. A nonincreasing sequence is bounded above. This means that all elements of the sequence must be less than a given real number. A nondecreasing sequence is bounded below. This means that all elements of the sequence must be greater than a given real number.

Discuss the sequence of partial sums, using the terms *converge*, *diverge*, and *sum of the series*.

Give the properties of the sum, difference, and scalar multiplication of convergent series.

Give the properties of a geometric series.

Explain the nth *term test for divergence*.

Define *sequence*.

Describe an *arithmetic sequence* using the terms *common difference* and *general term*.

To find the sum as n approaches infinity for the sum of two convergent series, find the sum as n approaches infinity for each individual series and add the results.

$$\sum_{n=1}^{\infty} (a_n + b_n) = \sum_{n=1}^{\infty} a_n + \sum_{n=1}^{\infty} b_n$$

To find the sum as n approaches infinity for the difference between two convergent series, find the sum as n approaches infinity for each individual series and subtract the results.

$$\sum_{n=1}^{\infty} (a_n - b_n) = \sum_{n=1}^{\infty} a_n - \sum_{n=1}^{\infty} b_n$$

To find the sum as n approaches infinity for the product of a scalar and a convergent series, find the sum as n approaches infinity for the series and multiply the result by the scalar.

$$\sum_{n=1}^{\infty} ka_n = k \sum_{n=1}^{\infty} a_n$$

Every infinite sequence of partial sums (infinite series) either converges or diverges. Like the test for convergence in a sequence, finding the limit of the sequence of partial sums will indicate whether it is a converging series or a diverging series. If there exists a real number S such that $\lim_{n \to \infty} S_n = S$, where S_n is the sequence of partial sums, then the series converges. If the limit equals infinity, then the series diverges. If $\lim_{n \to \infty} S_n = S$ and S is a real number, then S is also the convergence value of the series.

The **n^{th} term test for divergence** involves taking the limit of the nth term of a sequence and determining whether or not the limit is equal to zero. If the limit of the nth term is not equal to zero, then the series is a diverging series. This test only works to prove divergence, however. If the nth term is equal to zero, the test is inconclusive.

A **geometric series** is an infinite series in which each term is multiplied by a constant real number r, called the ratio. This is represented by the equation

$$\sum_{n=1}^{\infty} ar^{n-1} = a_1 + a_2 r + a_3 r^2 + \cdots + a_n r^{n-1} + \cdots.$$

If the absolute value of r is greater than or equal to one, then the geometric series is a diverging series. If the absolute value of r is less than one but greater than zero, the geometric series is a converging series. To find the sum of a converging geometric series, use the formula $\sum_{n=1}^{\infty} ar^{n-1} = \frac{a}{1-r}$, where $0 < |r| < 1$. If the series converges, it converges to zero. Otherwise, it diverges.

An **arithmetic sequence**, or arithmetic progression, is a special kind of sequence in which each term has a specific quantity, called the common difference, that is added to the previous term. The common difference may be positive or negative. The general form of an arithmetic sequence containing n terms is $a_1, a_1 + d, a_1 + 2d, \ldots, a_1 + (n-1)d$, where d is the common difference. The formula for the general term of an arithmetic sequence is $a_n = a_1 + (n-1)d$, where a_n is the term you are looking for and d is the common difference. To find the sum of the first n terms of an arithmetic sequence, use the formula $s_n = \frac{n}{2}(a_1 + a_n)$.

A sequence is a set of numbers that continues on in a define pattern. The function that defines a sequence has a domain composed of the set of positive integers. Each member of the sequence is an element, or individual term. Each element is identified by the notation a_n, where a is the term of the sequence, and n is the integer identifying which term in the sequence a is. There are two different ways to represent a sequence that contains the element a_n. The first is the simple notation $\{a_n\}$. The expanded notation of a sequence is $a_1, a_2, a_3, \ldots a_n, \ldots$. Notice that the expanded form does not end with the nth term. There is no indication that the nth term is the last term in the sequence, only that the nth term is an element of the sequence.

Describe a *geometric sequence* using the terms *common ratio* and *general term*.

Explain *unit circles* and *standard position*.

Identify which trigonometric functions are positive in each of the four quadrants.

Discuss the rectangular and polar coordinate system and explain how to convert between the two.

Define domain, range, and asymptotes as they relate to trigonometry.

Give the domain, range, and asymptotes of each of the six trigonometric functions.

A unit circle is a circle with a radius of 1 that has its center at the origin. The equation of the unit circle is $x^2 + y^2 = 1$. Notice that this is an abbreviated version of the standard equation of a circle. Because the center is the point $(0, 0)$, the values of h and k in the general equation are equal to zero and the equation simplifies to this form.

Standard Position is the position of an angle of measure θ whose vertex is at the origin, the initial side crosses the unit circle at the point $(1, 0)$, and the terminal side crosses the unit circle at some other point (a, b).

In the standard position, $\sin \theta = b$, $\cos \theta = a$, and $\tan \theta = \frac{b}{a}$.

A **geometric sequence**, or geometric progression, is a special kind of sequence in which each term has a specific quantity, called the common ratio, multiplied by the previous term. The common ratio may be positive or negative. The general form of a geometric sequence containing n terms is $a_1, a_1 r, a_1 r^2, \ldots, a_1 r^{n-1}$, where r is the common ratio. The formula for the general term of a geometric sequence is $a_n = a_1 r^{n-1}$, where a_n is the term you are looking for and r is the common ratio. To find the sum of the first n terms of a geometric sequence, use the formula $s_n = \frac{a_1(1 - r^n)}{1 - r}$.

Rectangular coordinates are those that lie on the square grids of the Cartesian plane. They should be quite familiar to you. The polar coordinate system is based on a circular graph, rather than the square grid of the Cartesian system. Points in the polar coordinate system are in the format (r, θ), where r is the distance from the origin (think radius of the circle) and θ is the smallest positive angle (moving counterclockwise around the circle) made with the positive horizontal axis.

To convert a point from rectangular (x, y) format to polar (r, θ) format, use the formula (x, y) to $(r, \theta) \Rightarrow r = \sqrt{x^2 + y^2}$; $\theta = \arctan \frac{y}{x}$ when $x \neq 0$

If x is positive, use the positive square root value for r. If x is negative, use the negative square root value for r.

If x = 0, use the following rules:
If x = 0 and y = 0, then $\theta = 0$
If x = 0 and y > 0, then $\theta = \frac{\pi}{2}$
If x = 0 and y < 0, then $\theta = \frac{3\pi}{2}$

To convert a point from polar (r, θ) format to rectangular (x, y) format, use the formula (r, θ) to $(x, y) \Rightarrow x = r \cos \theta$; $y = r \sin \theta$.

In the first quadrant, all six trigonometric functions are positive (sin, cos, tan, csc, sec, cot).
In the second quadrant, sin and csc are positive.
In the third quadrant, tan and cot are positive.
In the fourth quadrant, cos and sec are positive.
If you remember the phrase, "ALL Students Take Classes," you will be able to remember the sign of each trigonometric function in each quadrant. ALL represents all the signs in the first quadrant. The "S" in "Students" represents the sine function and its reciprocal in the second quadrant. The "T" in "Take" represents the tangent function and its reciprocal in the third quadrant. The "C" in "Classes" represents the cosine function and its reciprocal.

The domain, range, and asymptotes for each of the trigonometric functions are as follows:
In the sine function, the domain is all real numbers, the range is $-1 \leq y \leq 1$, and there are no asymptotes.
In the cosine function, the domain is all real numbers; the range is $-1 \leq y \leq 1$, and there are no asymptotes.
In the tangent function, the domain is $x \in$ all real numbers; $x \neq \frac{\pi}{2} + k\pi$, the range is all real numbers; and the asymptotes are the lines $x = \frac{\pi}{2} + k\pi$.
In the cosecant function, the domain is $x \in$ all real numbers; $x \neq k\pi$, the range is $(-\infty, -1] \cup [1, \infty)$, and the asymptotes are the lines $x = k\pi$.
In the secant function, the domain is $x \in$ all real numbers; $x \neq \frac{\pi}{2} + k\pi$, the range is $(-\infty, 1] \cup [1, \infty)$, and the asymptotes are the lines $x = \frac{\pi}{2} + k\pi$.
In the cotangent function, the domain is $x \in$ all real numbers; $x \neq k\pi$, the range is all real numbers, and the asymptotes are the lines $x = k\pi$.

In each of the above cases, k represents any integer.

The domain is the set of all possible real number values of x on the graph of a trigonometric function. Some graphs will impose limits on the values of x.
The range is the set of all possible real number values of y on the graph of a trigonometric function. Some graphs will impose limits on the values of y.
Asymptotes are lines which the graph of a trigonometric function approaches but never reaches. Asymptotes exist for values of x in the graphs of the tangent, cotangent, secant, and cosecant. The sine and cosine graphs do not have any asymptotes.

Give the measure in radians of each of the following angles: 0°, 30°, 45°, 60°, and 90°.
Give the sine, cosine, tangent, cosecant, secant, and cotangent of each of the angles.

Describe the graph of the sine function with a period of 360° or 2π radians.

Describe the graph of the cosine function with a period of 360° or 2π radians.

Describe the graph of the tangent function with a period of 180° or π radians.

List the trigonometric reciprocal, ratio, trigonometric, and cofunction identities.

Explain how to find the sine, cosine, or tangent of the sum or difference of two angles.

The sine (sin) function has a period of 360° or 2π radians. This means that its graph makes one complete cycle every 360° or 2π. Because $\sin 0 = 0$, the graph of $y = \sin x$ begins at the origin, with the x-axis representing the angle measure, and the y-axis representing the sine of the angle. The graph of the sine function is a smooth curve that begins at the origin, peaks at the point $\left(\frac{\pi}{2}, 1\right)$, crosses the x-axis at $(\pi, 0)$, has its lowest point at $\left(\frac{3\pi}{2}, -1\right)$, and returns to the x-axis to complete one cycle at $(2\pi, 0)$.

$0° = 0$ radians, $30° = \frac{\pi}{6}$ radians, $45° = \frac{\pi}{4}$ radians, $60° = \frac{\pi}{3}$ radians, and $90° = \frac{\pi}{2}$ radians

$\sin 0° = 0$	$\cos 0° = 1$	$\tan 0° = 0$
$\sin 30° = \frac{1}{2}$	$\cos 30° = \frac{\sqrt{3}}{2}$	$\tan 30° = \frac{\sqrt{3}}{3}$
$\sin 45° = \frac{\sqrt{2}}{2}$	$\cos 45° = \frac{\sqrt{2}}{2}$	$\tan 45° = 1$
$\sin 60° = \frac{\sqrt{3}}{2}$	$\cos 60° = \frac{1}{2}$	$\tan 60° = \sqrt{3}$
$\sin 90° = 1$	$\cos 90° = 0$	$\tan 90° =$ undefined
$\csc 0° =$ undefined	$\sec 0° = 1$	$\cot 0° =$ undefined
$\csc 30° = 2$	$\sec 30° = \frac{2\sqrt{3}}{3}$	$\cot 30° = \sqrt{3}$
$\csc 45° = \sqrt{2}$	$\sec 45° = \sqrt{2}$	$\cot 45° = 1$
$\csc 60° = \frac{2\sqrt{3}}{3}$	$\sec 60° = 2$	$\cot 60° = \frac{\sqrt{3}}{3}$
$\csc 90° = 1$	$\sec 90° =$ undefined	$\cot 90° = 0$

The values in the upper half of this table are values you should have memorized or be able to find quickly.

tangent (tan) function has a period of 180° or π radians, which means that its graph makes one complete cycle every 180° or π radians. The x-axis represents the angle measure, and the y-axis represents the tangent of the angle. The graph of the tangent function is a series of smooth curves that cross the x-axis at every 180° or π radians and have an asymptote every $k \cdot 90°$ or $\frac{k\pi}{2}$ radians, where k is an odd integer. This can be explained by the fact that the tangent is calculated by dividing the sine by the cosine, since the cosine equals zero at those asymptote points.

The cosine (cos) function has a period of 360° or 2π radians, which means that its graph also makes one complete cycle every 360° or 2π. Because $\cos 0° = 1$, the graph of $y = \cos x$ begins at the point $(0, 1)$, with the x-axis representing the angle measure, and the y-axis representing the cosine of the angle. The graph of the cosine function is a smooth curve that begins at the point $(0, 1)$, crosses the x-axis at the point $\left(\frac{\pi}{2}, 0\right)$, has its lowest point at $(\pi, -1)$, crosses the x-axis again at the point $\left(\frac{3\pi}{2}, 0\right)$, and returns to a peak at the point $(2\pi, 1)$ to complete one cycle.

To find the sine, cosine, or tangent of the sum or difference of two angles, use one of the following formulas:
$$\sin(\alpha \pm \beta) = \sin\alpha \cos\beta \pm \cos\alpha \sin\beta$$
$$\cos(\alpha \pm \beta) = \cos\alpha \cos\beta \mp \sin\alpha \sin\beta$$
$$\tan(\alpha \pm \beta) = \frac{\tan\alpha \pm \tan\beta}{1 \mp \tan\alpha \tan\beta}$$
where α and β are two angles with known sine, cosine, or tangent values as needed.

To take the reciprocal of a number means to place that number as the denominator of a fraction with a numerator of 1.
The trigonometric reciprocal identities are $\csc\theta = \frac{1}{\sin\theta}$; $\sec\theta = \frac{1}{\cos\theta}$; and $\cot\theta = \frac{1}{\tan\theta}$.

The trigonometric ratio identities are: $\tan\theta = \frac{\sin\theta}{\cos\theta}$ and $\cot\theta = \frac{\cos\theta}{\sin\theta}$.
The Pythagorean Theorem states that $a^2 + b^2 = c^2$. The trigonometric identities that have this same format are: $\sin^2\theta + \cos^2\theta = 1$, $\tan^2\theta + 1 = \sec^2\theta$, and $\cot^2\theta + 1 = \csc^2\theta$.
The trigonometric cofunction identities use the trigonometric relationships of complementary angles (angles whose sum is 90°). These are: $\sin x = \cos(90° - x)$, $\sec x = \csc(90° - x)$, $\tan x = \cot(90° - x)$, $\cos x = \sin(90° - x)$, $\csc x = \sec(90° - x)$, and $\cot x = \tan(90° - x)$.

College-Level Math
© Mometrix Media - flashcardsecrets.com/accuplacer

Explain how to find the sine and cosine of half of a known angle.

Explain how to find the tangent and cotangent of half of a known angle.

College-Level Math
© Mometrix Media - flashcardsecrets.com/accuplacer

College-Level Math
© Mometrix Media - flashcardsecrets.com/accuplacer

Explain how to find the sine, cosine, tangent, and cotangent of twice a known angle.

Explain how to find the product of the sines and cosines of two angles.

College-Level Math
© Mometrix Media - flashcardsecrets.com/accuplacer

College-Level Math
© Mometrix Media - flashcardsecrets.com/accuplacer

Explain the differences between solving trigonometric equations and algebraic equations.

Define the six inverse trigonometric functions.

To find the tangent or cotangent of half of a known angle, use the following formulas:

$$\tan\frac{\theta}{2} = \frac{\sin\theta}{1+\cos\theta}$$
$$\cot\frac{\theta}{2} = \frac{\sin\theta}{1-\cos\theta}$$

where θ is an angle with known exact sine and cosine values. These formulas will work for finding the tangent or cotangent of half of any angle unless the cosine of θ happens to make the denominator of the identity equal to 0.

To find the sine or cosine of half of a known angle, use the following formulas:

$$\sin\frac{\theta}{2} = \pm\sqrt{\frac{1-\cos\theta}{2}}$$

$$\cos\frac{\theta}{2} = \pm\sqrt{\frac{1+\cos\theta}{2}}$$

where θ is an angle with a known exact cosine value. To determine the sign of the answer, you must notice the quadrant the given angle is in and apply the correct sign for the trigonometric function you are using. If you need to find the exact sine or cosine of an angle that you do not know, such as sin 22.5°, you can rewrite the given angle as a half angle, such as $\sin\frac{45°}{2}$, and use the formula above.

To find the product of the sines and cosines of two different angles, use one of the following formulas:

$$\sin\alpha\sin\beta = \frac{1}{2}[\cos(\alpha-\beta) - \cos(\alpha+\beta)]$$
$$\cos\alpha\cos\beta = \frac{1}{2}[\cos(\alpha+\beta) + \cos(\alpha-\beta)]$$
$$\sin\alpha\cos\beta = \frac{1}{2}[\sin(\alpha+\beta) + \sin(\alpha-\beta)]$$
$$\cos\alpha\sin\beta = \frac{1}{2}[\sin(\alpha+\beta) - \sin(\alpha-\beta)]$$

where α and β are two unique angles.

In each case, use one of the Double Angle Formulas. To find the sine or cosine of twice a known angle, use one of the following formulas:

$$\sin(2\theta) = 2\sin\theta\cos\theta$$
$$\cos(2\theta) = \cos^2\theta - \sin^2\theta \text{ or}$$
$$\cos(2\theta) = 2\cos^2\theta - 1 \text{ or}$$
$$\cos(2\theta) = 1 - 2\sin^2\theta$$

To find the tangent or cotangent of twice a known angle, use the formulas:

$$\tan(2\theta) = \frac{2\tan\theta}{1-\tan^2\theta}$$
$$\cot(2\theta) = \frac{\cot\theta - \tan\theta}{2}$$

In each case, θ is an angle with known exact sine, cosine, tangent, and cotangent values.

Each of the trigonometric functions accepts an angular measure, either degrees or radians, and gives a numerical value as the output. The inverse functions do the opposite; they accept a numerical value and give an angular measure as the output. The inverse sine, or arcsine, commonly written as either $\sin^{-1}x$ or arcsin x, gives the angle whose sine is x. Similarly:

The inverse of cos x is written as $\cos^{-1}x$ or arccos x and means the angle whose cosine is x.

The inverse of tan x is written as $\tan^{-1}x$ or arctan x and means the angle whose tangent is x.

The inverse of csc x is written as $\csc^{-1}x$ or arccsc x and means the angle whose cosecant is x.

The inverse of sec x is written as $\sec^{-1}x$ or arcsec x and means the angle whose secant is x.

The inverse of cot x is written as $\cot^{-1}x$ or arccot x and means the angle whose cotangent is x.

Trigonometric and algebraic equations are solved following the same rules, but while algebraic expressions have one unique solution, trigonometric equations could have multiple solutions, and you must find them all. When solving for an angle with a known trigonometric value, you must consider the sign and include all angles with that value. Your calculator will probably only give one value as an answer, typically in the following ranges:

For the inverse sine function, $\left[-\frac{\pi}{2},\frac{\pi}{2}\right]$ or [–90°, 90°]

For the inverse cosine function, $[0, \pi]$ or [0°, 180°]

For the inverse tangent function, $\left[-\frac{\pi}{2},\frac{\pi}{2}\right]$ or [–90°, 90°]

It is important to determine if there is another angle in a different quadrant that also satisfies the problem. To do this, find the other quadrant(s) with the same sign for that trigonometric function and find the angle that has the same reference angle. Then check whether this angle is also a solution.

Define De Moivre's Theorem.

Describe the Slope-Intercept Formula.

Describe the calculation for Intercept.

Describe the formula for Slope.

Describe a triangle.

Define the following geometrical terms: line, line segment, parallel lines, perpendicular lines, and ray.

Slope-Intercept Form

Linear functions describe straight lines and have the general form
$$y = f(x) = mx + b$$
The number m is called the slope and determines the tilt of the line, while b is called the y-intercept, the point on the y-axis where the line crosses at x = 0. This form of a linear equation is often called slope-intercept form. A typical graph of one of these functions looks like this:

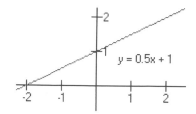

$y = 0.5x + 1$

De Moivre's Theorem is used to find the powers of complex numbers (numbers that contain the imaginary number i) written in polar form. Given a trigonometric expression that contains i, such as $z = r \cos x + ir \sin x$, where r is a real number and x is an angle measurement in polar form, use the formula $z^n = r^n(\cos nx + i \sin nx)$, where r and n are real numbers, x is the angle measure in polar form, and i is the imaginary number $i = \sqrt{-1}$. The expression $\cos x + i \sin x$ can be written cis x, making the formula appear in the format $z^n = r^n$ cis nx.
Note that De Moivre's Theorem is only for angles in polar form. If you are given an angle in degrees, you must convert to polar form before using the formula.

Slope

The slope is calculated from knowing any two distinct points on the line, (x_1, y_1) and (x_2, y_2)

$$m = \frac{y_2 - y_1}{x_2 - x_1}$$

If the points are distinct, then the x coordinates cannot be the same and so zeros in the denominator are avoided.

Intercept

The y-intercept can be calculated from any point if the slope is known. Since for any point (x_1, y_1)

$$y_1 = mx_1 + b$$

we must then have

$$b = y_1 - mx_1 = y_1 - \frac{y_2 - y_1}{x_2 - x_1} x_1$$

Line: straight line extending indefinitely in both directions
Line segment: has two endpoints
Parallel lines: two non-intersecting lines in the same plane
Perpendicular lines: two intersecting lines forming four angles of 90° each
Ray: has a single endpoint and extends indefinitely from that point

The sum of the measures of the angles of a triangle is 180°.
Equilateral triangles – each angle is 60°; all 3 sides are equal.

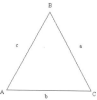

Isosceles triangles have two angles and sides that are equal.

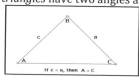

If c = a, then A = C

Discuss volume.

Discuss units of measure.

Discuss surface area.

Discuss the Pythagorean theorem.

Discuss supplementary angles.

Discuss complementary angles.

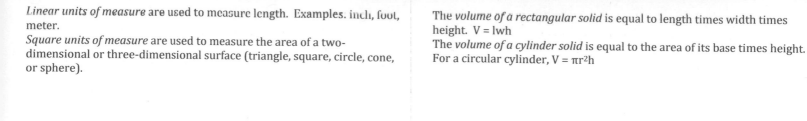

Linear units of measure are used to measure length. Examples: inch, foot, meter.
Square units of measure are used to measure the area of a two-dimensional or three-dimensional surface (triangle, square, circle, cone, or sphere).

The *volume of a rectangular solid* is equal to length times width times height. $V = lwh$
The *volume of a cylinder solid* is equal to the area of its base times height. For a circular cylinder, $V = \pi r^2 h$

In right triangles, the sum of the squares of the sides equals the square of the hypotenuse.
The *hypotenuse* is the side opposite the right angle.
$a^2 + b^2 = c^2$
Example: Triangle ABC has the following dimensions: Side A = 3; Side B = 2. What is side C, or the hypotenuse?
$3^2 + 4^2 = 5^2$
$9 + 16 = 25$
Side C, or the hypotenuse = 25.

Surface area is the total area of all outside surfaces of a three-dimensional object. To calculate surface area, the area of each side, or outside surface, must be computed; these are summed to determine the total surface area.

Two angles are *complementary* if their sum equals 90°.
Example: Angles a & b in the diagram below combine to form a 90° angle therefore they are called complementary angles.

Two angles are *supplementary* if their sum is 180°, or a straight line.
Example: Angles a & b in the diagram below combine to form a 180° angle, or straight line; these are called supplementary angles.

Discuss straight angles, obtuse angles, and acute angles.

Describe the basics of Alternate Interior Angles.

Describe the basics of naming angles.

Describe the basics of Corresponding Angles.

Describe the area and perimeter of a square.

Describe the area and perimeter of a rectangle.

Alternate Interior Angles

For any pair of parallel lines 1 and 2, that are both intersected by a third line, such as line 3 in the diagram below, angle A and angle D are called alternate interior angles. Alternate interior angles have the same degree measurement. Angle B and angle C are also alternate interior angles.

Straight angle - An angle measuring exactly 180°.
Obtuse angle - An angle measuring between 90 and 180°.
Acute angle - An angle measuring less than 90°.

Corresponding Angles

For any pair of parallel lines 1 and 2, that are both intersected by a third line, such as line 3 in the diagram below, angle A and angle C are called corresponding angles. Corresponding angles have the same degree measurement. Angle B and angle D are also corresponding angles.

We can specify an angle by using a point on each ray and the vertex. The angle below may be specified as angle ABC or as angle CBA; you may also see this written as $\angle$ ABC or as $\angle$ CBA. Note how the vertex point is always given in the middle.

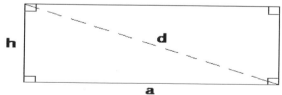

Area and Perimeter of Rectangle

$$d = \sqrt{a^2 + h^2}$$

$$a = \sqrt{d^2 - h^2}$$

$$h = \sqrt{d^2 - a^2}$$

Perimeter$= 2a + 2h$

Area$= a * h$

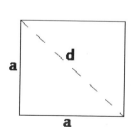

Area and Perimeter of Square

$$d = a\sqrt{2}$$

Perimeter$= 4a = 2d\sqrt{2}$

Area$= a^2 = \frac{1}{2}d^2$

Describe the area and volume of a sphere.

Describe the basics of an isosceles triangle.

Describe the basics of an obtuse triangle.

Describe the area and perimeter of a circle.

Describe the area and volume of a cube.

$3/24 \div (-2/3) = ?$

a) -16/3
b) -3/16
c) -1/12
d) 3/16
e) 1/12

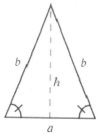

An *isosceles triangle* is a triangle with (at least) two equal sides. In the figure above, the two equal sides have length b and the remaining side has length a. This property is equivalent to two angles of the triangle being equal. An isosceles triangle therefore has both two equal sides and two equal angles. The name derives from the Greek iso (same) and skelos (leg). A triangle with all sides equal is called an equilateral triangle, and a triangle with no sides equal is called a scalene triangle. The height of the isosceles triangle illustrated above can be found from

the Pythagorean theorem as $h = \sqrt{b^2 - \frac{1}{4}a^2}$

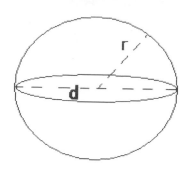

Area and Volume of Sphere

$d = 2r$

$A_{surface} = 4\pi r^2$

$Volume = \frac{4}{3}\pi r^3$

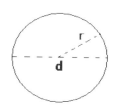

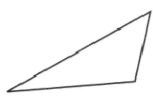

An *obtuse triangle* is a triangle in which one of the angles is an obtuse angle. (Obviously, only a single angle in a triangle can be obtuse or it wouldn't be a triangle.) A triangle must be obtuse, acute, or right.

Area and Perimeter of Circle

$d = 2r$

$Perimeter = 2\pi r = \pi d$

$Area = \pi r^2$

b) -3/16
When dividing fractions, the simplest way to solve the problem is to take the second number, the divisor, which in this case is (-2/3) and invert it. Then multiply the two numbers. That gives 3/24 * -3/2. Multiplying that out results in -9/48, which reduces down to -3/16, by dividing both the numerator and denominator by a common factor of 3.

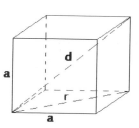

Area and Volume of Cube

$r = a\sqrt{2}$

$d = a\sqrt{3}$

$Area = 6a^2$

$Volume = a^3$

$0.9837 = ?$
a) 983.7×10^3
b) 0.009837×10^3
c) 9.873×10^{-1}
d) 9837.0×10^{-5}
e) 0.09837×10^{-1}

Heidi must divide 870 bales of hay between three stables so that the second has 90 bales more than the first, but 150 less than the third. How many bales does the third stable receive?
a) 180
b) 270
c) 310
d) 420
e) none of these

Solve for y : $y/2 - y/3 - 2 = 0$
a) -2
b) 5/12
c) 2
d) 12/5
e) 12

$(-2)^3 - (-2)^2 = ?$
a) 4   b) -2   c) -4   d) -10   e) -12

$(-3)(-8) + 6/-2 - 3 = ?$
a) -30   b) -12   c) 4   d) 6   e) 18

Let c = 3 and d = 7. Evaluate 20 – 2c + 4d.
a) 14
b) 18
c) 22
d) 42
e) 54

d) 420

Equations need to be set up based on the word problem.

X = 1st stable

Y = 3rd stable

90+x = 2nd stable; y-150 = the 2nd stable

90+x= y-150 This is determined from the statement "the second has 90 bales more than the first, but 150 less than the third."

We will solve for y.

90+x=y-150

90+x+150=y

x+240=y

Now, we can substitute for y. Our equation will be the 1st stable + the 2nd stable + the 3rd stable = 870 bales of hay.

X + (90+x) + (x+240) = 870.

X+90+x+x+240=870

X+x+x = 870-240-90

3x = 540

x = 540/3 = 180. Therefore, y = x+240 = 180+240 = 420 bales of hay, which is answer choice d.

c) 9.873×10^{-1}

Scientific notation is used due to the belief that it is easier to read exponents than it is to read zeros. Scientific notation uses negative exponents for numbers that are less than one.

In the number .9837, scientific notation can easily be used by moving the decimal point one place to the right. For one decimal point being moved, we use scientific notation with 10^{-1}. Therefore, .9837 becomes 9.873×10^{-1}.

e) -12

$(-2)^3 - (-2)^2 = ?$

$(-2*-2*-2) - (-2*-2) = ?$

$(-8) - (4) = ?$

$-8 - 4 = -12$

e) 12

This equation can be solved by determining a common denominator for each term in the equation. We have the terms y/2, y/3, and 2. 2 has an implied denominator of 1. So, we need to find a common denominator for the denominators 1, 2, and 3. The lowest common denominator would be 6; 1, 2, and 3 can all be divided into 6. 6 can be divided by 2 a total of 3 times, so we multiply the numerator, y, by 3; therefore y/2 becomes 3y. 6 can be divided by 3 a total of 2 times, so we multiply the numerator, y, by 2; therefore, y/3 becomes 2y. 6 can be divided by 1 (the implied denominator of the whole number 2) 6 times, so we multiply 2 times 6; therefore, our 2 becomes a 12. So, our new equation is 3y - 2y - 12 = 0. We will put our unknowns on the left side of the equation and our known numbers on the right side of the equation, so we have 3y-2y = 0+12. 1y = 12. 12 divided by 1 equals 12, so our answer is solution e, which is 12.

d) 42

Let c = 3 and d = 7. Evaluate 20 - 2c + 4d

20-2(3) + 4(7) = ?

20 - 6 + 28 = 42

e) 18

$(-3)(-8) + (-6/2) - 3 = 24 + (-3) - 3$

24-3-3 = 18

Simplify :

$$\left(\frac{m^2 - x^2}{m^2 + mx}\right)\left(\frac{m^2 - x^2}{m^2 + mx}\right)$$

a) x

b) $\dfrac{(m-x)^2}{m^2}$

c) –x

d) –x/m

e) $\dfrac{m+x}{m} \dfrac{m+x}{m}$

Solve for x : x + 4/3 = -20/3
a) -72
b) -46/3
c) -8
d) 16/3
e) 8

Solve for s : s/4- 7/2= 4
a) 11
b) 14
c) 16
d) 30
e) none of these

Which of the following is a factorization of the polynomial $2x^2 + x - 6$?
a) $2(x^2 + x - 3)$
b) $(2x + 2)(x - 3)$
c) $(2x + 3)(x - 2)$
d) $(2x - 3)(x + 2)$
e) $(2x + 6)(x - 1)$

$(2(2x^2 - 3y)\ (7y - x) = ?$
a) $2x^2 - 21xy + x$
b) $-2x^3 + 14x^2y + 3xy - 21y^2$
c) $-2x^3 + 14x^2y + 24xy$
d) $7x^2y - 23x3y^2 + 3y$
e) $12xy - 21y^2 + 3xy$

Penny can knit 4 rows of a sweater in 5 minutes. How many hours will it take her to knit 300 rows?
a) 4
b) 6¼
c) 12½
d) 240
e) 375

c) -8

x + 4/3 = -20/3. We will isolate the unknown and solve.

X = -20/3 – 4/3

X = -24/3 = -8

$$\frac{(m-x)^2}{m^2}$$

b) We must first factor the polynomials. We will first examine the numerator in the 1st polynomial. $(m^2-x^2) = (m-x)(m+x)$. Denominator in the 1st polynomial. $(m^2+mx) = m(m+x)$. Therefore, the first polynomial can be factored into the following: $[(m-x)(m+x)]/[m(m+x)]$. We will cancel out like terms in the numerator and the denominator to simplify. As there is an $(m+x)$ term in both, we will cancel that out. Therefore, the resulting polynomial becomes $(m-x)/m$. The numerator in the 2nd polynomial, $(m^2-x^2) = (m+x)(m-x)$. The denominator in the 2nd polynomial, $(m^2+mx) = m(m+x)$. The resulting polynomial is $[(m+x)(m-x)]/ m(m+x)$. We will cancel out like terms in the numerator and the denominator to simplify. As there is an $(m+x)$ term in both, we will cancel that out. Therefore, the resulting polynomial becomes $(m-x)/m$. Since both polynomials resulted in $(m-x)/m$, our answer will be $(m-x)^2 / m^2$.

d) $(2x - 3)(x +2)$

We will factor the polynomial, $2x^2 + x – 6$, by determining the greatest common factor of the polynomial. The first term of each binomial multiplied together will equal $2x^2$, the 1st term of the polynomial. Multiplying the last term of the 1st binomial with the first term of the 2nd binomial will equal $-3x$. Multiplying the first term of the first binomial and the last term of the last binomial will equal $4x$. Adding the $-3x$ and the $4x$ will equal x, the 2nd term of the polynomial. Finally, multiplying the last term of each binomial will equal -6, the last term of the polynomial.

d) 30

s/4 – 7/2 = 4 We will determine a common denominator, isolate the unknown, and solve. Our denominators are 4, 2, and 1 (implied denominator of the whole number 4). s/4 has a denominator of 4, so multiplying it by 4 will cancel the denominator and will become s. For the term 7/2, 2 will go into 4 a total of 2 times, so we will multiply 7 times 2, which will become 14. The term 4 will be multiplied by 4 and will become 16.

Now, our equation is s – 14 = 16

S= 16+14

S = 30

b) 6¼

We can set up a proportion to solve. Our first ratio in the proportion will be 4/5 since 4 rows can be knitted in 5 minutes. Our second ratio in the proportion will be 300/x since we are trying to determine the length of time it will take to knit 300 rows. Note that the number of rows is the numerator and the lenthg of time is the denominator for both ratios. We will cross-multiply the ratios and solve for x.

4/5 = 300/x

4x = 300(5)

4x = 1500

x = 375 minutes

375/60 minutes = 6¼ hours

b) $-2x^3+14x^2y + 3xy – 21y^2$

$(2x^2-3y) (7y – x)$ We will factor using the foil method (see the FOIL method flashcard for further detail).

We will first multiply the first term of each: $2x^2 * 7y = 14x^2y$

Next, multiply the last term of the 1st polynomial and the 1st term of the 2nd polynomial: $-3y*7y = -21y^2$

Multiply the 1st term of the 1st polynomial and the last term of the 2nd polynomial: $2x^2 * -x = -2x^3$

Multiply the last term of each polynomial: $-3y * -x = 3xy$

Combine all terms in the appropriate order: $-2x^3 + 14x^2y + 3xy -21y^2$

The center of a circle is (0,-1). What is the area of the circle if it passes through the point (0,5)?
a) 16π
b) 9π
c) 12π
d) 36π
e) 3π

The points (5,2), (6,5), and (X,-4) are collinear. What is the value of X?
a) -1
b) 0
c) 1
d) 2
e) 3

Points A(-3,-4) and B(7,-2) determine line segment AB in the standard (x,y) coordinate place. If the midpoint of AB is (a,-3), what is the value of a?
a) 2
b) -4
c) 4
d) -5
e) 5

What is the slope of the line joining (-3,6) and (-4,0)?
a) 6
b) 1/6
c) -6
d) -7/6
e) 6/7

In which quadrant(s) are points (X,Y) located if (X,Y) satisfies the equation XY = 6?
a) I and II
b) II & IV
c) I & III
d) II & III
e) I & IV

The diagram represents the graph of what set of numbers?

a) integers $\geq$ -2 and $\leq$ 1}
b) {real numbers > -2 and < 1}
c) {real numbers between -2 and 1}
d) {integers between -2 and 1, inclusive}
e) {real numbers between -2 and 1, inclusive}

e) 3
First you should solve for the slope of the line.
m = (y2-y1)/(x2-x1) = (5-2)/(6-5) = 3/1 = 3
Next you should solve for b (the y-intercept) in the formula y = mx + b, and using the first point (5,2) you know that y = mx + b or 2 = 3(5) + b, which results in b = 2 − 15 or -13
Using the equation y = mx + b, and plugging in the known variables, you have -4 = 3(x) − 13 which simplifies to 3(x) = 9 or x =3.

d) 36π
According to the problem, the circle center passes through (0, -1); the circle also passes through (0,5). This gives us the distance, along the y-axis, of the circle from the center to the circle; this is defined as the radius. The circle goes from -1 to 5, which would be 6 units; this is the radius.
The area of a circle = πr².
Area = π6²
Area = 36π

a) 6
The slope is calculated from knowing any two distinct points on the line, (x_1, y_1) and (x_2, y_2)

$$m = \frac{y_2 - y_1}{x_2 - x_1}$$

(-3,6) and (-4,0)
m = (0-6)/[(-4)-(-3)]
m = -6/(-4+3)
m = -6/(-1)
m = 6

a) 2
Points A(-3,-4) and B(7,-2)
First, subtract the leftmost endpoint's x coordinate from the rightmost endpoint's x coordinate 7 - -3 = 7+3 = 10. Then divide by two, 10/2 = 5. Then add that number to the leftmost x coordinate -3 + 5 = 2, which is the midpoint's x coordinate.

E) {real numbers between -2 and 1, inclusive}
The process of elimination can be used on this problem. The black line includes all the numbers between -2 and -1 and so you know that the answer can't be either of the choices that state "integers". Then, you have to have an answer choice that includes the two extreme numbers on the line, which are -2 and 1, and not just the numbers in between them. Only choice E is inclusive of points -2 and 1.

c) I & III
Since the product of X and Y is a positive number, X and Y must either both be positive numbers, or they must both be a negative number. If they are both positive numbers, then they lie in quadrant I. If they are both negative numbers, then they lie in quadrant III.

The distance between points (5,2) & (1,-1) is:
a) √5
b) √17
c) 5
d) √37
e) 9

What is the length of the diagonal of the square whose vertices are A(-4,-1), B(-3,3), C(1,2), D(0,-2)?
a) 6
b) √34
c) 8
d) 4
e) √10

In isosceles triangle A(-2,-2), B(-4,4), C(2,6), AB = BC. What are the coordinates of the point where the altitude meets the base AC?
a) (-2,5)
b) (3,1)
c) (2,4)
d) (0,2)
e) (-3,1)

The slope of the tangent to a circle at (4,5) is -2/3. What are the coordinates of the center of the circle?
a) (1,7)
b) (5,4)
c) (-2,3)
d) (2,2)
e) (1,4)

How far is the point (-3,-4) from the origin?
a) 2√3
b) √17
c) √22
d) 5
e) 7

Charles, Bob, Mary, Ted, Sue and Bill want to play checkers. How many different two-person games can be played?
a) 3
b) 5
c) 15
d) 30
e) 72

b) $\sqrt{34}$

You must first determine the square side length by using the distance formula between any 2 sets of points. Since it's a square, all sides have the same length. Using (-4,-1) and (-3,3):

$\sqrt{[(x_1-x_2)^2 + (y_1-y_2)^2]}$
$\sqrt{[\{-4-(-3)\}^2 + \{-1-(3)\}^2]}$
$\sqrt{[(-1)^2 + (-4)^2]}$
$\sqrt{[1 + 16]}$
$\sqrt{17}$ = each square side length

If a diagonal is drawn in the square, two triangles are created. The square diagonal is the triangle hypotenuse, so Pythagorean's Theorem can be used to determine the hypotenuse (or square diagonal) length.

$a^2 + b^2 = c^2$
$\sqrt{17}^2 + \sqrt{17}^2 = c^2$
$17 + 17 = c^2$
$34 = c^2$
$\sqrt{34} = c$

c) 5

(5,2) (1,-1)
$\sqrt{[(x_1-x_2)^2 + (y_1-y_2)^2]}$
$\sqrt{[(5-1)^2 + \{2-(-1)\}^2]}$
$\sqrt{[(4)^2 + (2+1)^2]}$
$\sqrt{[16 + (3)^2]}$
$\sqrt{(16 + 9)}$
$\sqrt{25}$
$=5$

d) (2,2)

Like with many problems, the simplest way to approach this one is to draw a picture first. Draw a simple graph and plot the point (4,5), along with a line of slope -2/3 going through that line. The quickest way to plot a slope is to take the numerator of the slope fraction and go up or down that much, then take the denominator and count right that much to find the next point on the line. With two points on the line, you can draw the line. Once you have the tangential line, then you know the center of the circle is going to lie on the line that is perpendicular to the tangential line. If the tangential line has a slope -2/3, then the line containing the center will have a slope 3/2, and will also pass through point (4,5). Now you've redefined the problem to be, "Which point lies on the line with slope 3/2, which passes through point (4,5)?" Only choice d, (2,2) satisfies that criteria.

d) (0,2)

As this is an isosceles triangle, the sides and angles opposite the sides are equal. The altitude would meet the base at the midpoint of AC. The A coordinates are (-2,-2), and the C coordinates are (2,6). The midpoint formula should be used:

$[(x_1 + x_2)/2], [(y_1 + y_2)/ 2]$
$[(-2 + 2)/2], [(-2 + 6)/ 2]$
$(0/2), (-2 + 6)/ 2$
0, 2 answer choice d

c) 15

This can be determined by looking at the two-person game options:
1. Charles & Bob
2. Charles & Mary
3. Charles & Ted
4. Charles & Sue
5. Charles & Bill
6. Bob & Mary
7. Bob & Ted
8. Bob & Sue
9. Bob & Bill
10. Mary & Ted
11. Mary & Sue
12. Mary & Bill
13. Ted & Sue
14. Ted & Bill
15. Sue & Bill
The answer is 15, answer choice c.

d) 5

The origin is located at (0,0). The distance from point (-3,-4) to (0,0) needs to be determined using the following distance formula.

$\sqrt{[(x_1-x_2)^2 + (y_1-y_2)^2]}$
$\sqrt{[(-3-0)^2 + (-4-0)^2]}$
$\sqrt{[(-3)^2 + (-4)^2]}$
$\sqrt{(9 + 16)}$
$\sqrt{25}$
$= 5$

A deck of 52 playing cards with 13 cards in each suit – clubs, diamonds, hearts and spades – is shuffled. What is the probability of picking a card at random and getting a heart or a club?
a) 1/26
b) 1/13
c) 2/13
d) 1/4
e) 1/2

What is the probability of tossing a fair coin three times and getting the outcome head, tail, head, in that order?
a) 1/8
b) 1/7
c) 1/2
d) 3/7
e) 1/128

How many different five-digit automobile license plate numbers may be formed if 0 may not be used for the first or the fifth digit?
a) $2^9 \times 2^{10} \times 2^{10} \times 2^{10} \times 2^9$
b) $9^2 \times 10^2 \times 10^2 \times 10^2 \times 9^2$
c) $10 \times 9 \times 10 \times 10 \times 8$
d) $10 \times 9 \times 8 \times 7 \times 6$
e) $9 \times 10 \times 10 \times 10 \times 9$

When the science group containing six children leaves the main class once a week for special instruction, the science teacher lines up the students and leads them to the science room. How many different ways can the teacher line up the six children?
a) 15
b) 30
c) 36
d) 720
e) 46,656

A fair coin is tossed seven times. On the first six tosses, the coin comes up: head, tail, head, tail, head, tail. What is the probability that the coin will come up a head on the seventh toss?
a) 1/128
b) 1/7
c) 1/2
d) 3/7
e) 127/128

If 2 dice are tossed, what is the probability that their sum will be odd?
a) 1/4
b) 1/2
c) 18/37
d) 5/36
e) 5/18

a) 1/8
To find the answer, you should note that order is important. To flip the first coin and get a "head" outcome, is a probability of 1/2. To flip the next coin and get a "tail" outcome is a probability of 1/2. To flip the last coin and get a "head" outcome, is a probability of 1/2. Multiplying those together produces $1/2*1/2*1/2 = 1/8$, or choice A.

e) ½
There are 26 cards that are either a heart or a club. There are 52 cards total. 26/52 = 1/2, answer choice e.

d) 720
This is a factorial problem.
$6! = 6 * 5 * 4 * 3 * 2 * 1$
$6! = 720$, answer choice d.

e) 9 x 10 x 10 x 10 x 9
There are 10 numbers that can be used from 0-9. For the 1st and 5th digit, there are nine numbers that can be used from 1-9. Therefore, answer choice e is correct.

b) ½
When 2 die are tossed, the resulting sum will be either even or odd. There is a 50% chance of either. Therefore, there is a 50%, or ½ chance of the resulting sum being odd; answer choice b is correct.

c) 1/2
For every individual coin toss, there is a 50% chance that it will land on a head. The preceding coin tosses have no effect on the following coin toss. Therefore, there is a 50%, or ½ chance that the 7th coin toss will land on a head; answer choice c is correct.

A line passes through (4,5) and its slope is 2. What is the equation of the line?
a) y = 2x + 3
b) y = 3x + 2
c) y = 2x – 3
d) y = 3x – 2

The slope of the line whose equation is 4x + 5y = 20 is?
a) 4/5
b) -4/5
c) 4
d) -4
e) 5/4

The lines y = 3 and x = 6 intersect at what point?
a) (3,6)
b) (6,3)
c) (0,0)
d) (3,0)
e) (0,3)

What is the solution set for the system of equations represented by the graph?

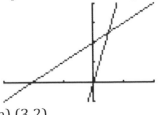

a) (3,2)
b) (1,3)
c) (3,1)
d) (5/2, 1/2)
e) (1/2, 5/2)

What is the x-intercept of 3y – 6 = 2x?
a) (-3,0)
b) (3,0)
c) (6,3)
d) (6,0)
e) (0,-6)

Which system of equations has no common solution?
a) x – y = 7   b) 3x – 2y = 5   c) y = 4x + 1
   2x = 2y + 14   x + 2y = 4   y = 4x + 3

h) -4/5

To determine the slope of the line for the equation $4x + 5y = 20$, we will use the slope-intercept formula. (See the slope-intercept formula flashcard for more detail.)

The slope-intercept formula is $y=mx+b$. mx is the slope; b is the intercept. We will put our equation into this form and solve for y.

$4x + 5y = 20$

$5y = -4x + 20$

$y = -4/5x + 4$

Therefore, the slope is -4/5.

c) $y = 2x - 3$

We must substitute the coordinate points and solve to determine the y-intercept. The coordinate points are (4,5). The slope is 2.

$Y = mx + b$

$5 = (2)(4) + b$

$5 = 8 + b$

$5-8 = b$

$-3 = b$ The y-intercept is -3

$y = mx + b$

$y = 2x -3$, answer choice c.

e) (1/2, 5/2)

The solution set can be determined from examining the graph at the point of intersection between the two lines. Looking at the x-axis the point of intersection appears to be between 1 and 2, probably around halfway between the two points. Looking at the y-axis, the point of intersection appears to be between 2 and 3, probably around halfway between the two points. So, the point of intersection appears to be at (½, 2 ½), which is equal to answer choice e.

b) (6,3)

When graphing points on a graph, the coordinates are given. The x coordinate is always given before the y coordinate. As the problem says, x=6 and y=3; therefore, the coordinates are (6,3).

c) $y = 4x + 1$ $y = 4x + 3$

Each of the answer choice pairs should be solved to find a solution.

$x - y = 7$ $2x = 2y + 14$

$x = 7 + y$

$2(7+y) = 2y + 14$

$14+2y=2y+14$

$2y-2y=14-14$

$0y=0, y=0$

$x=7+y=7+0=7$

$x-y=7$

$7-0=7, 7=7$

$3x - 2y = 5$ $x + 2y = 4$

$x = 4-2y$

$3(4-2y) - 2y = 5$

$12-6y - 2y = 5$

$-8y = 5-12$

$y = 7/8$, $x=4 - 2y = 4 - 2(7/8) = 2 1/4$

$y = 4x +1$ $y = 4x + 3$ Just by looking at the structure of these equations, it is obvious there is no common solution. The equations contradict one another. However, you can attempt to solve; there is no common solution.

a) (-3,0)

The x-intercept occurs when y=0. So plugging in y=0 into the given equation, you have $3(0) - 6 = 2x$. This reduces to $2x = -6$ or $x = -3$. That makes (-3,0) or choice a correct.

The conversion formula to change degrees Fahrenheit (F) to degrees Celsius (C) is :
C = A(F – B)
If C = 0 when F = 32 and C = 100 when F = 212, then what is the value of A?
a) 0
b) 1.8
c) 5/9
d) 9
e) 18

What is the slope of a line joining (-4, 7) and (-5, 0)?
a) 7
b) 1/7
c) -7
d) -9/7
e) 7/9

What is the equation of a line parallel to y = -2x + 5 and passing through (0, -3) ?

a) y = -2x – 3
b) y = 2x – 3
c) y = -2x – 1/3
d) y = -2x + 3
e) y = 2x + 1/3

What is the equation of the line passing through (-2,1) and having a slope of ½?
a) ½(x-2) = y-1
b) y = ½ x + 2
c) y = 2x + ½
d) y = x + 2
e) y = -2x

Which of the following ordered pairs (x,y) will satisfy the equation x – y = xy?
     I. (0,0)   II. (2,1)   III. (1,1)   IV. (1,-1)
a) I only
b) II only
c) I & II only
d) III only
e) I, II, III and IV

Solve the following system of equations for x :
4x – y = 1
2x + 2y = 3
a) -2
b) -½
c) ½
d) 2/3
e) 2

a) 7

To determine the slope, we must use the slope calculation formula. (See the slope calculation flashcard for further detail.) Slope calculation is: $m = [(y_2-y_1)/(x_2-x_1)]$ The x and y coordinates presented in the problem will be used in this formula.

(-4, 7) and (-5, 0)

$m = \{[(0)-(7)]/[(-5)-(-4)]\}$

$m = [(0-7)/(-5+4)]$

$m = (-7)/(-1)$

$m = -7/-1$

$m = 7$

---

c) 5/9

You have two unknowns and you can quickly solve for B, by plugging in C = 0 when F = 32 into the equation. This gives you 0 = A(32-B), which turns into 0 = 32A – BA, which is equal to BA = 32A, which means B = 32. Now you have using the other equation 100 = A(212 – 32). This gives you 100 = 180A. Solving this gives you A = 100/180 or 5/9, which is choice c.

---

b) $y = \frac{1}{2} x + 2$

Using the coordinates given (-2,1) and the given slope(1/2) , we can solve for x.

y = mx + b

$y = \frac{1}{2}x + b$

$1 = \frac{1}{2} (-2) + b$

$1 = (-1) + b$

$1+1 = b$

$2 = b$, the y-intercept

$y = \frac{1}{2}x + 2$, answer choice b.

---

a) y = -2x – 3

The problem states that the lines are parallel, which dictates that the slopes will be the same. So, the slope will remain -5. The coordinates given, (0,-3) notes that the y-intercept will be -3. Therefore, choice a is correct.

---

c) ½

4x – y = 1

2x + 2y = 3

We will isolate the unknown to one equation in order to solve the other equation.

4x – y = 1

-y = 1 - 4x

y = -1 + 4x

Now we will solve the 2nd equation by substituting for y.

2x + 2y = 3

2x + 2 (-1 + 4x) = 3

2x -2 + 8x = 3

2x + 8x = 3 + 2

10x = 5

x = 5/10

x = 1/2

---

a) I only

This problem can be solved by attempting to solve the equation with each solution set. From the problem, the solution sets are: (0,0), (2,1), (1,1), and (1,-1),

x-y=xy

0-0=0(0)

0=0 Solution set I solves the equation.

x-y=xy

2-1=2(1)

1=2 Solution set II does not solve the equation.

x-y=xy

1-1=1(1)

0=1 Solution set III does not solve the equation.

x-y=xy

1-(-1) = 1(-1)

2=-1 Solution set IV does not solve the equation.

Which of the following systems of equations does not have a solution?

a) $x + 3y = 7$
   $3x - y = 9$

b) $3x - y = 2$
   $x - 3y = 1$

c) $x + 3y = 8$
   $x - 3y = 6$

d) $x - 3y = 4$
   $3x - 9y = 1$

e) $x - 3y = 7$
   $3x + y = 9$

What is the slope of $y = 3$? Of $x = -1$?
a) 0; -1
b) 0; ∞
c) 0; 1
d) ∞ ; 1
e) 1; -1

How many units long is 1 side of a square with perimeter 20c – 12 units?
a) 20c – 12
b) 20c – 3
c) 8c
d) 5c – 12
e) 5c – 3

In the figure, if AB is a straight line and m∠CDB = 60°, what is the measure of ∠CDA?

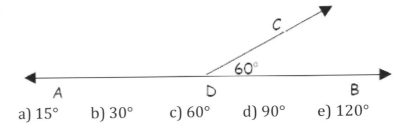

a) 15°   b) 30°   c) 60°   d) 90°   e) 120°

Describe the basics of Parallel lines.

Describe the formula for area and perimeter calculations with a triangle.

b) 0; ∞

y = 3 on a graph would be a horizontal line. Horizontal lines have a slope of 0.

x = -1 on a graph would be a vertical line. Vertical lines have no slope.

d) x – 3y = 4   3x – 9y = 1

You should try to solve each of the answer choice pairs and see if you can find a solution. a.) Substituting the first equation x + 3y = 7, where x = 7 – 3y, into the second equation, gives you 3(7 – 3y) – y = 9. This becomes 21 – 9y – y = 9, which equals 21 – 10y = 9, which equals 10y = 12, or y = 5/4. b.) Substituting the first equation 3x – y = 2, where x = (2 + y)/3, into the second equation, gives you (2 + y)/3 – 3y = 1. Multiplying both sides by three gives you 2 + y – 9y = 3, which equals 2 – 8y = 3, which equals 8y = -1 or y = -1/8.

c.) Substituting the first equation x + 3y = 8, where x = 8 – 3y, into the second equation, gives you (8 – 3y) – 3y = 6. This becomes 8 – 6y = 6, which equals 6y = 2, or y = 1/3. d.) Substituting the first equation x – 3y = 4, where x = 4 + 3y, into the second equation, gives you 3(4 + 3y) – 9y = 1. This becomes 12 + 9y – 9y = 1, which equals 12 = 1, which is invalid, meaning that choice D doesn't have a solution. e.) Substituting the first equation x – 3y = 7, where x = 7 + 3y, into the second equation, gives you 3(7 + 3y) + y = 9. This becomes 21 + 9y + y = 9, which equals 21 + 10y = 9, which equals 10y = -12, or y = -6/5.

e) 120°

We know that a straight line has 180°. We will set up an equation to determine the measure of ∠CDA.

X + 60 = 180

X = 180-60

X = 120

e) 5c – 3

We are given the total perimeter of a square as 20c-12. All four sides of a square are equal. Therefore, we can divide the total perimeter by 4 to determine the length of each side. 20c/4 = 5c. 12/4 = 3. Therefore, the length of one square side is 5c-3.

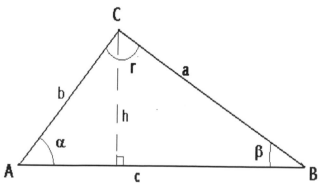

Area = ½ Base x Height
Perimeter = Side a + Side b + Side c

Parallel lines have the same slope.
y = 3x + 5
y = 3x - 7
y = 3x + 0.5
y = 3x + 2
These lines are ALL parallel.
They all have the same slope (m).
(Remember y = mx + b.)
Perpendicular lines have negative reciprocal slopes.

The height of a rectangular solid is 4 meters greater than its width. Its length is 2m less than 3 times its width. Which represents the volume of the solid in cubic meters?
a) w(3w-2)(w+4)
b) w(3w-2)(w-4)
c) 2(3w+2)(w+4)
d) w(3w+2)(w-4)
e) 3w(w-2)(w+4)

A rectangle tank having dimensions of 1 meter by 2 meters by 4 meters contains 4 cubic meters of water. When the tank is placed level on its various sides, the water depth changes. What is the greatest possible difference in water depths?
a) .5m
b) 1m
c) 1.5m
d) 2m
e) 3m

If two-thirds of the perimeter of an equilateral triangle is 6, what is its perimeter?
a) 4
b) 8
c) 9
d) 12
e) 18

If a rectangle has a perimeter of 14 and a length of 4, what is its area?
a) 3
b) 4
c) 12
d) 24
e) none of the above

What is the volume of a square box with a side length of 8?
a) 16
b) 512
c) 64
d) 24
e) 32

A right triangle with legs of 7 inches and 24 inches has a perimeter of:
a) 31
b) 56
c) 84
d) 168
e) none of these

c) 1.5m

The depths for each different tank configuration need to be determined. If 1 meter is the height, then the bottom of the tank will be 2 x 4, meaning that the water level will be .5 meters, because 2x4 = 8 cubic meters of water is what it would take to get a water level of 1 meter, and you only have 4 cubic meters, so 4/8 = .5 If 2 meters is the height, then the bottom of the tank will be 1 x 4, meaning that the water level will be 1 meter, because 1x4 = 4 cubic meters of water is what it would take to get a water level of 1 meter and that is exactly what you have. If 4 meters is the height, then the bottom of the tank will be 1 x 2, meaning that the water level will be 2 meters, because 1x2 = 2 cubic meters of water is what it would take to get a water level of 1 meter, and you have twice that, or 4 cubic meters of water, and so 2/1 = 2

Thus, the greatest possible difference between the three possibilities of .5, 1, and 2 is given by 2 - .5 = 1.5, or choice c.

d) $w(3w-2)(w+4)$

Height = w + 4
Length = 3w – 2
Volume = width * length * height
Volume = w (3w-2) (w+4)

c) 12

Perimeter, or P = 14
Length, or L = 4
Width = W
Area = A
2L + 2W = 14
2 (4) + 2W = 14
8 + 2W = 14
2W = 14-8
2W = 6
W = 3
Area = LW
A = 4(3)
A = 12

c) 9

Perimeter = 3 * sides
P = 3s
2/3 (P) = 6
P = 6/(2/3)
P = 9

b.)   56

Side a = 7; Side b = 24

We will first determine the length of the hypotenuse in the right triangle, then we will calculate the perimeter from the length of the three sides. We can use the Pythagorean Theorem to determine the length of the hypotenuse. The Pythagorean Theorem is $a^2 + b^2 = c^2$. The a and b represent the two sides; c represents the hypotenuse. To calculate the perimeter, we will add all the sides together.

$a^2 + b^2 = c^2$
$7^2 + 24^2 = c^2$
$49 + 576 = c^2$
$625 = c^2$
$c = 25$
P = s+s+s
P = 7 + 24 + 25
P = 56

b) 512

$V = s^3$
$V = 8^3$
V = 512

Three points R, S and T are collinear. Point S lies between R and T. If RS = 2/3 RT and RS = 48, find ½ RT.
a) 72
b) 60
c) 48
d) 36
e) 24

Points E, F and G are collinear. If EF = 8 and EG = 12, which point cannot lie between the other 2?
a) E
b) F
c) G
d) F & G
e) cannot be determined

If PRQ is a straight line, find the number of degrees in ∠w.

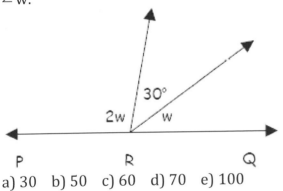

a) 30   b) 50   c) 60   d) 70   e) 100

Line XY is perpendicular to line CD at D. Which conclusion can be drawn?
a) XD = DY
b) XY = CD
c) m∠XDC = 90°
d) m∠XDC = 90° and XD = DY
e) all of the above

If the hypotenuse of a right triangle is 8 inches long and 1 acute angle measure 60°, 1 leg must have a length, in inches, of:
a) $2\frac{2}{3}$
b) 4
c) $4\sqrt{2}$
d) 6
e) $6\sqrt{3}$

The length of a side of a square is $4\sqrt{2}$. What would be the length of the square's diagonal?
a) 4
b) $4\sqrt{2}$
c) 8
d) $8\sqrt{2}$
e) 16

c) G

Line Segment EF is 8 units long; Line Segment EG is 12 units long. Therefore, Point G could not be in the middle of E and F. The length of Line Segment EG exceeds the length of Line Segment EF, so therefore point G could not be in the middle.

d) 36
RS = 2/3 RT
RS = 48
2/3 RT = 48
RT = 72
½ RT = ½ (72) = 36

c) m $\angle$ XDC = 90°
By definition, perpendicular lines are two intersecting lines forming four angles of 90° each. Therefore, $\angle$ XDC would have 90°.
Choices a, b, and d are not necessarily accurate since line segment lengths are not given.

b) 50
We know that a straight line has 180°. We will set up an equation to determine the degrees in $\angle$ w.
2w + 30 + w = 180
3w = 180-30
3w = 150
w = 50

c) 8
We can use Pythagorean's Theorem to determine the length of the diagonal. (See the Pythagorean Theorem flashard for more details.) We are given the length of one side of the square. Since we are considering a square, all four sides have the same length. If we drew a diagonal through the square, we will be making 2 right triangles within the square.
We have two side lengths each of $4\sqrt{2}$.
$A^2 + b^2 = c^2$
$(4\sqrt{2})^2 + (4\sqrt{2})^2 = c^2$
32 + 32 = c^2
64 = c^2
8=c
8 is the length of the hypotenuse, or the square diagonal.

b) 4
If a right triangle has an angle of 30° and an angle of 60°, the side that is across, or opposite from the 30° angle is equal to ½ the length of the hypotenuse. According to the problem, we have one an angle of 30°, which means we have an angle of 60°, since this is a right triangle and triangles has 180°. Since the hypotenuse is 8 units long, then the side opposite the 30° angle, will be ½ (8), or 4 units long.

Three equal semi-circles are drawn on the diameter of the circle with center Q as in the diagram. If the area of circle Q is 9π, find the area of the shaded region.

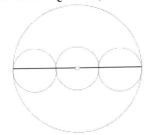

a) 7π/2   b) 3π   c) 9π/2   d) 5π   e) 11π

Find the area of a sector of a circle if the sector has a central angle of 90° and a radius of 2.
a) 1
b) π
c) 2π
d) 4π
e) 8

In the figure, find the area of the entire region formed by triangle ABC and the semicircle having AB as its diameter.

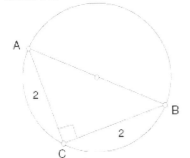

a) 2 + π   b) 2 + 2π   c) 1 + π   d) 4 + 4 π   e) 2 + 4π

A regular hexagon has a side of length 2. If the hexagon is inscribed in a circle, what is the area of the circle?
a) π
b) π²
c) 2π²
d) 4π
e) 4π²

In the figure, if the small circle has a radius R, and the larger circle has a diameter 6R, what is the area of the region inside the large circle and outside the small circle?

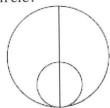

a) π/2   b) 3πR/4   c) πR/2   d) 8πR²   e) 15πR²

In the figure below, RS is tangent to circle O. If PO is 5 and QR is 8, what is the value of RS?

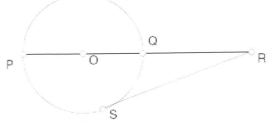

a) 5   b) √39   c) 8   d) 12   e) 144

b) π

A circle sector area = (the central angle/360°) (circle area)

Circle area = $\pi r^2 = \pi 2^2 = = 4\pi$

Central angle = 90°

(90/360) (4π)

= (1/4) (4π)

= π, answer choice b

b) 3π

According to the problem, the area of the big circle is 9π and that Area = πr^2. The square root of 9 is 3, which means the radius of the big circle must be 3; therefore, the diameter is equal to 6. If the diameter of the big circle is 6, the diameters of the smaller circles must be 2, because 6/3 = 2 and there are 3 smaller circles along the big diameter.

If the smaller circles have a diameter of 2, then they have a radius of 1, which means the area of the smaller circles is $\pi 1^2$, which is just π. There are three smaller circles, each with area of π, so their total area is given by 3π.

d) 4π

Begin by drawing a hexagon with a circle around it on scratch paper to understand what it looks like. Starting from one of the hexagons vertexes, draw as many internal triangles as you can inside of the hexagon. You should be able to draw 4. That means there are 4*180 = 720 degrees in a hexagon. 720/6 vertexes = 120 degrees on each vertex. You are trying to find the length across the farthest two points of the hexagon. In drawing the internal triangles earlier, you should have drawn a right triangle, whose hypotenuse is the distance between the farthest points, whose acute angle is 30 degrees, and whose opposite leg is length 2, making the hypotenuse length 4. That is the diameter of the circle, and since Area = πr^2, Area = $\pi (4/2)^2$ or 4π, which is choice d.

a) 2 + π

For the area of the triangle, A = ½bh, where b = base and h = height. The base and height of the triangle are both 2 units.

A = 1/2 (2)(2)

A = ½ (4)

A = 2

Pythagorean's Theorem can be used to determine the length of AB, which is the diameter of the circle. AB is the triangle's hypotenuse.

$A^2 + b^2 = c^2$

$2^2 + 2^2 = c^2$

$4 + 4 = c^2$

$8 = c^2$

$\sqrt{8} = c$, the hypotenuse length and the diameter length. Therefore, the radius = $(\sqrt{8})/2$

Area of a semicircle = $(\pi r^2)/2$

$A = [(\pi)(\sqrt{8}/2)^2]/2$

A = π

Therefore, the triangle area = 2 and the area of the semicircle = π.

d) 12

When you first look at this problem, it appears that there are lots of things not given; however, they can be deduced. The length of PO, OQ, and OS are all the same, which is 5. OS and SR form a 90 degree angle. To get the length of the hypotenuse, add the length of OQ and QR, which is 5 + 8 = 13. You need to know the length of RS. SOHCAHTOA means that the sine of angle ORS is given by 5/13. The inverse sine of 5/13 is 22.6, which means the angle of ORS is 22.6 degrees. Now you know the cosine ORS is equal to length SR/13. The cosine of 22.6 degrees is equal to SR/13. Cosine (22.6) = .923 Multiplying .923*13 = 12, to solve for length SR, which is choice d.

d) 8πR²

In order to answer the question, you have to figure out the area of the big circle and the area of the smaller circle. The big circle has a diameter of 6R, which means it would have a radius of 3R. Area = πr^2; therefore, the big circle would have an area of $\pi(3R)^2$, which is equal to $9\pi R^2$. The smaller circle has a radius R, which means it has an area of πR^2. $9\pi R^2 - \pi R^2 = 8\pi R^2$, which is choice d.

What is the perimeter of a square inscribed in a circle whose circumference is 6π?
a) 18
b) √12/2
c) 12√2
d) 24√2
e) 4√12

A regular polygon of N sides is inscribed in a circle. If each intercepted arc measures 30°, how many sides does the polygon have?
a) 8
b) 10
c) 12
d) 30
e) cannot be determined

In the rectangle, PQ=X and QR=2X. What percent of the perimeter of the rectangle is the sum of PQ + QR + RS?

a) 50%   b) 66 2/3%   c) 75% d) 80%   e) 83 1/3%

If the measure of each interior angle in a regular polygon is 90°, how many sides does the polygon have?
a) 3
b) 4
c) 6
d) 8
e) 12

In the figure, isosceles, right triangle AEF overlaps square ABCD as shown. If AB = 1 and FA = 4, what is the area of EFCD?

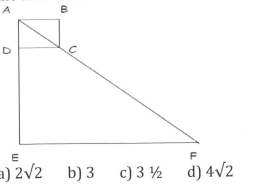

a) 2√2   b) 3   c) 3 ½   d) 4√2   e) 8

If arc AB is one-fourth of the circumference of a certain circle and if the length of the chord AB is x, what is the diameter of the circle?

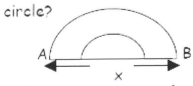

a) √2x   b) πx / 4   c) x√2   d) 4x /π   e) 2x√2

a) 12

Polygons have a total of 360°. If each intercepted arc is 30°, the polygon would have 12 sides. 360/20 = 12.

c) $12\sqrt{2}$

The formula for circumference of a circle is πd, with d being the length of the diameter. In this case, the diameter of the circle is equal to the diagonal of the square, which is 6.

Now you are trying to find the perimeter of a square, whose diagonal is 6. Since the corners of a square are 90 degrees, then you know that the two triangles formed by the diagonal are 45-45-90 degree triangles. Using the Pythagorean theorem, and setting the length of a side to a, you have $a^2 + a^2 = c^2$, or $2a^2 = 36$. Solving for a you get $a = \sqrt{18}$, which is the same as $\sqrt{(2*9)}$ or $3\sqrt{2}$. Since there are 4 sides, to find the perimeter you have $4*3\sqrt{2}$ or $12\sqrt{2}$, which is choice c.

b) 4

Polygons have a total of 360°. If all angle are 90°, there are 4 side. 360/90 = 4 sides.

b) 66 2/3%

PQ = x

QR = 2x

IF PQ = x, then RS = x. If QR = 2x, then SP = 2x. The total perimeter would be x + x + 2x + 2x = 6x.

QP + QR + RS = x + x + 2x = 4x

4x/6x = 2/3 = 66 2/3%

c) $x\sqrt{2}$

The simplest way to visualize this is to draw it out. Once you draw out what the whole circle would look like, you realize that the entire circle could contain a square, and one edge of that square would be represented by chord AB. The diagonal of that square would be equal to the diameter of the circle.

Now you have a new problem. What is the diagonal of a square with side length x? The Pythagorean theorem would state $x^2 + x^2 = y^2$, or $2x^2 = y^2$, or $y = \sqrt{2x^2}$ or $y = x\sqrt{2}$, which is choice c.

c) 3 ½

AB = 1

FA = 4

For isosceles right triangle, AEF, the area needs to be determined. The hypotenuse length is 4. In a hypotenuse triangle, the hypotenuse length is equal to the hypotenuse length times $\sqrt{2}$. The hypotenuse length is 4; the other sides' length is $4/\sqrt{2}$, or 2.83.

A = ½bh

A = ½ (2.83) (2.83)

A = 4

For triangle ABC, or triangle ACD, the side length is 1. Since these are isosceles triangles, the hypotenuse length is $\sqrt{2}$. Triangle ACD area should be computed:

A = 1/2bh

A = ½ (1) (1)

A = ½

4 – 1/2 = 3 ½, answer choice c.

If the perimeter of square A is half the perimeter of square B, then the area of square B is how many times the area of square A?

a) ½
b) 1
c) 2
d) 3
e) 4

In the diagram below, a car starts at point A and travels 13 miles east, then 12 miles north, and finally 4 miles west to point D. If the car traveled a straight path from D to A., how many miles would this trip be?

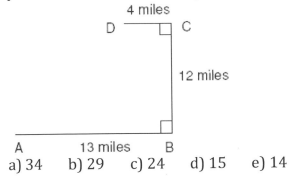

a) 34   b) 29   c) 24   d) 15   e) 14

The area of a rectangular floor is 170 square feet. The length of the floor is 3 feet less than twice the width. How many feet wide is the floor?

a) 8.5
b) 10
c) 14
d) 15
e) 17

The ratio of the angles in a triangle is 1:2:3. What would the new ratio be if the smallest angle is doubled and the largest one remains the same?

a) 1:1:3
b) 1:2:3
c) 2:1:3
d) 2:2:2
e) 2:2:3

A recipe for 7 cups of barbecue sauce requires 5 tablespoons of vinegar. If Susan has only 3 tablespoons of vinegar but wants to follow the recipe, how many cups of barbecue sauce can she make with this recipe?

a) 2
b) 2 4/5
c) 3 4/5
d) 4 1/5
e) 5 1/5

A student has earned scores of 72, 81, 88 and 68 on each of 4 tests. To receive an average (arithmetic mean) grade of 80, what score must she earn on the fifth and final test?

a) 3
b) 11
c) 78
d) 80
e) 91

d) 15

If an imaginary line is drawn from point D straight down to Line Segment AB, a rectangle is formed with side lengths of 4 and 12. We will call the point on AB, point E.

If an imaginary line is drawn from point D to point A, a right triangle is formed with Line Segment AD, Line Segment AE, and Line Segment DE. We know Line Segment AE is 9 miles long; AB was 13 miles long. When the rectangle was formed, EB became 4 miles long, which means AE is 9 miles long. Line Segment DE is 12 miles long, since a rectangle was formed and Line Segment BC is 12 miles long. Using Pythagorean's Theorem, we can calculate the length of the hypotenuse.

$A^2 + b^2 = c^2$

$9^2 + 12^2 = c^2$

$81 + 144 = c^2$

$225 = c^2$

$\sqrt{225} = c^2$

$15 = c$, answer choice d.

e) 4

This problem can best be solved by using assigning numbers to the problem. Perimeter of square A = 4, or half the perimeter of square B. The perimeter of a square formula is P = 4s. The s stands for side length. Therefore, Square A sides are 1 unit in length each. Perimeter of square B = 8. From the perimeter of a square formula, we can determine that Square B sides are 2 units in length each.

Area of square A = $s^2 = 1^2 = 1$

Area of square B = $s^2 = 2^2 = 4$

4/1 = 4. Therefore, the area of square B is 4 times the area of square A. Answer choice e is correct.

c) 2:1:3

The ratio presented in the problem is 1:2:3. If the smallest angle is doubled, the 1 will become a 2. If the largest angle remains the same, it will remain a 3. To keep the total ratio accurate, the middle angle must remain the same, so the 2 remains a 2. So, our answer is 2:1:3.

b) 10

L = 2w-3

Area = w x L = 170

w x (2w-3) = $2w^2$ – 3w = 170

$2w^2$ – 3w -170 = 0

(2w + 17)(w – 10) = 0

w -10 = 0

w = 10

L = 2w – 3 = 2(10) – 3 = 20 – 3 = 17

You need to find the width, which is 10, making choice b correct.

e) 91

(72 + 81 +88 + 68 + x)/5 = 80

(309 + x)/5 = 80

To eliminate the denominator on the left side of the equal sign, multiply both sides by 5. The right side of the equal sign will become 400.

309 + x = 400

x = 400-309

x = 91

d) 4 1/5

This can be solved by setting up ratios of barbeque sauce to vinegar. Cross-multiply and solve for x.

7/5 = x/3

5x = 7(3)

5x = 21

x = 4 1/5

If 25% of a number is 120 less than 40% of the same number, what is the number?
a) 120
b) 250
c) 400
d) 800
e) 1,200

The sum of the squares of two numbers is 2 more than twice their product. If one of the numbers if 7, which of the following equations can be used to solve the other number?
a) $x^2 + 49 = 2x$
b) $x^2 + 49 = 2x + 2$
c) $x^2 + 49 = 14x + 2$
d) $x^2 + 49 = 2 - 14x$
e) $x^2 + 49 = 2 - 2x$

x is a real number and $16^x = 4^3$; what is the value of x?
a) ½
b) 3/2
c) 3
d) 4
e) 9

A television set cost a store $130. It is normally sold at a 50% retail markup. What profit will the store make if the retail price is discounted by 20%?
a) $65
b) $39
c) $30
d) $26
e) $20

The area of a circle is directly proportional to the square of its radius. If the radius is halved, by what factor is the area multiplied?
a) 1/8
b) 2
c) ½
d) 4
e) 1/4

In a certain city, one-fifth of the school year is 39 days. What portion of the school year would 26 days represent?
a) 1/15
b) 2/15
c) 7.5
d) 15
e) 1/3

c) $x^2 + 49 = 14x + 2$

Since we know that one of these numbers is 7, we will use that number. From the statement, "the sum of the squares of two numbers is two more than twice their product," which is $14x + 2$. $2*7 = 14$, which gives us the 14x. "two more" means that we should add 2 to the 14x. Therefore, the answer is choice c.

d) 800

An equation should be set up. Isolate and solve for the unknowns.

.25x = .4x – 120

120 = .15x

x = 800

d) $26

Cost = 130

Sale price = 130 (150%) This is due to the 50% markup.

Sale price = 130*1.5 = 195

Discounted price = 195 (80%) Due to the 20% discount from the retail sale price.

Discounted price = 156

156 Discounted price

Less: 130 Cost

= 26 Profit

b) 3/2

16 is the square of 4, and so another way to write $16^x = 4^3$ is to change it to: $4^{2x} = 4^3$

Now, you have the equation $2x = 3$, which means $x = 3/2$

b) 2/15

Solve to determine the number of days in the school year.

1/5x = 39

x = 39/(1/5)

x = 39*5

x = 195

Determine the portion of the school year that 29 days represent. Reduce to lowest terms.

26/195 Both are divisible by 13.

2/15

e) ¼

The simplest way to solve this type of problem is to plug in some examples. If you had a radius of 4, then its square is 16. If you halved that radius, cutting it down to 2, then the square of 2 is 4. So you've gone from 16 to 4, which is ¼ of the original size.

During an August heat wave, Wendy kept track of the high temperature every day for a week. She graphed her results on a line graph. To the nearest degree, what was the average high temperature that week?

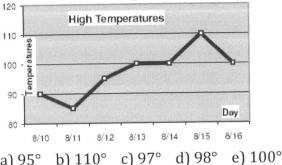

a) 95°   b) 110°   c) 97°   d) 98°   e) 100°

Mylin's Magic Club collects $4,000 from the sale of tickets when there is a full house. If all the tickets cost the same amount, how much money will Mylin collect from the purchase of tickets if the club is 75% full?
a) $2,000
b) $2,500
c) $3,000
d) $3,250
e) $3,500

Of the 1,450 students at Sampson College, 22% are sophomores. How many students are NOT sophomores?
a) 319
b) 659
c) 791
d) 1,131
e) 1,418

A salesperson is paid $100 per week plus 7% of the amount of her sales, s. Which equation could be used to find her weekly pay, p, in dollars?
a) $p = (1.07)^s$
b) $p = 1.07s$
c) $p = 100s + .07s$
d) $p = .07(100 + s)$
e) $p = 100 + .07s$

Steve saves 10 percent on a regularly priced $40 radio but still must pay 5 percent sales tax on the reduced price. What is the total amount that he must pay?
a) $41.80
b) $38.20
c) $38.00
d) $37.80
e) $35.00

The mode of 11 numbers ranging from 20 to 30 is 28. If there are four 23's, how many 28's are there?
a) 1
b) 2
c) 3
d) 4
e) 5

c) $3,000
4000 * 75% = 3,000, answer choice c.

c) 97°
First you need to add up all the numbers. 90 + 85 + 95 + 100 + 100 + 110 + 100 = 680. Then to find the average, divide the total by the number of records, 680/7 = 97 degrees, making choice c correct.

e) p = 100 + .07s
She is paid $100 per week. She is paid 7% of her sales, which is represented by .07s. The total pay is represented by p. Therefore, p = 100 .07s.

d) 1,131
If 22% of the students are sophomores, then 78% of the sophomores are not sophomores. There is a total of 1,450 students. 78% of 1,450 students = 1,131 students.

e) 5
There is a total of 11 numbers between 20 to 30. That means that one number is 20 and one number is 30. That leaves 9 numbers. There are 4 23's, which means there are 5 28's.

d) $37.80
10% of the price will be taken off. So, we will compute 90% of the total. 40 * 90% is $36. We will multiply by 105% to add 5% to the cost. $36*105% = $37.80.

Lucy made 9 out of 15 basketball free-throw shots. Ann made 18 of 25 basketball free-throw shots. What is the difference between Lucy's free-throw percentage and Ann's free-throw percentage?
a) 9%
b) 12%
c) 18%
d) 25%
e) 60%

Of the parts produced per hour by unit A of a factory, 20% are defective, 30% of the parts produced per hour by unit B are defective. If unit A produces 60% as many parts per hour as unit B, what is the average percent of defective parts per hour in the factory?
a) 55%
b) 26¼%
c) 25%
d) 23%
e) 15%

A driver traveled at 40 mph for two hours and 30 mph for one-half hour. What was his average rate of speed?
a) 38
b) 36
c) 35
d) 34
e) 32

What is the average of the odd integers from -7 to 99?
a) 53
b) 50
c) 48
d) 46
e) 40

What is the mode of the test scores in this class of 20 students?

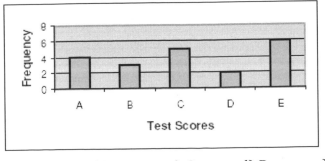

a) A   b) B   c) C   d) D   e) E

$$\frac{0.25 \times 10^2}{10^3} = ?$$
a) 0.025
b) 0.25
c) 2.5
d) 25.0
e) 250.0

b) 26¼%

The easiest way to determine the solution is to assign values in the problem.

A = 20% defective products per hour
B = 30% defective products per hour
B Total Production = 100
A Total Production = 60% (B) = 60%(100) = 60
Total production = 160
.2(A total production) + .3 (B total production) = total defective products per hour
.2(60) + .3(100) = 12 + 30 = 42
42 defective products/160 total production
42/160 = 26 ¼%, answer choice b.

b) 12%

We will calculate a fraction representing each of the girls' free-throw percentages, find a common denominator, and compute the difference between each of the girls' free-throw percentages.

Lucy = 9/15 = 3/5 = 15/25
Ann = 18/25
18/25 – 15/25 = 3/25 = 12%

d) 46

If you add all odd integers from -7 to 99, the total is 2,484. To compute the average, divide the number of values. In this case, there are 54 total values. 2,484/54 = 46, which is answer choice d.

a) 38

We will break down the trip into ½ hour increments since part of our information is given in a ½ hour increment. The first information was given as 40 mph for 2 hours, which is 4 30-minute increments. We will then divide to compute the average of the 5 30-minute increments.
40 + 40 +40 40 + 30 = 190.
190/5 = 38 average mph

a) 0.025

.25 x 100 = 25. 25/1000 = .025. Therefore, solution a is the correct answer.

e) E

Mode is the most frequent value in a set of data. In the graph, the E column has the highest frequency. Therefore, answer choice e is correct.

If A = (1,6) & B = (5,2), what is the midpoint of $\overline{AB}$?
a) (6,8)
b) (3,4)
c) (4,3)
d) (8,6)
e) (3,1)

If the slope of one leg of a right triangle is ½, then the slope of the other leg must be:
a) -2
b) 1/2
c) -1/2
d) 2/3
e) 2

On a true-false test with three questions, what is the probability of guessing the answers to exactly two questions correctly?
a) 2/3
b) 3/8
c) 1/2
d) 5/8
e) 3/4

U, V, W and X are collinear. $\overline{UX}$ is 50 units long. $\overline{UW}$ is 22 units long and $\overline{VX}$ is 29 units long. How many units long is $\overline{VW}$?
a) 1
b) 7
c) 7.5
d) 21
e) 28

Analyze the use of headings and subheadings.

Describe the use of bold text and underlining.

a) -2

It might be easier for you to draw this out and see it visually, but the slope of a line perpendicular to another line with slope x, will be given by -1/x. In this case, a slope of 1/2, will be perpendicular to a line with slope -2/1 or -2.

b) (3,4)

A = (1,6) & B = (5,2), what is the midpoint of $\overline{AB}$?
First, subtract the leftmost endpoint's x coordinate from the rightmost endpoint's x coordinate 5 - 1 = 4. Then divide by two, 4/2 = 2. Then add that number to the leftmost x coordinate 1 + 2 = 3, which is the midpoint's x coordinate.
Second, subtract the lower endpoint's y coordinate from the higher endpoint's y coordinate 6 – 2 = 4. Then divide by two, 4/2 = 2. Then add that number to the lower y coordinate 2 + 2 = 4, which is the midpoint's y coordinate. So the midpoint is given by (3 , 4)

a) 1

U, V, W and X are collinear. $\overline{UX}$ is 50 units long. $\overline{UW}$ is 22 units long and $\overline{VX}$ is 29 units long.
If Line Segment UW is subtracted from Line Segment UX, or 22 is subtracted from 50, we can determine that Line Segment WX is 28 units. If Line Segment UV and Line Segment WX is subtracted from Line Segment UX, the remaining Line Segment VW is 1 unit.

b) 3/8

Since there are only three questions, you can fairly easily write out all eight possibilities and then count up how many satisfy the requirement. With "R" denoting a right answer, and "W" denoting a wrong answer, the possibilities are: RRR, RWR, RRW, RWW, WRR, WWR, WRW, WWW. Looking over these eight possibilities, there are three different ways that you could get exactly two questions correctly, meaning 3/8 is the correct answer, or b.

Authors will often incorporate text features like bold text, italics, and underlining to communicate meaning to the reader. When text is made bold, it is often because the author wants to emphasize the point that is being made. Bold text indicates importance. Also, many textbooks place key terms in bold. This not only draws the reader's attention, but also makes it easy to find these terms when reviewing before a test. Underlining serves a similar purpose. It is often used to suggest emphasis. However, underlining is also used on occasion beneath the titles of books, magazines, and works of art. This was more common when people used typewriters, on which italics are not possible. Now that word processor software is more prevalent, italics are generally used for longer works.

Many informative texts, especially textbooks, use headings and subheadings for organization. Headings and subheadings are typically printed in larger and bolder fonts, and are often in a different color than the main body of the text. Headings may be larger than subheadings. Also, headings and subheadings are not always complete sentences. A heading announces the topic that will be addressed in the text below. Headings are meant to alert the reader to what is about to come. Subheadings announce the topics of smaller sections within the entire section indicated by the heading. So, for instance, the heading of a section in a science textbook might be *AMPHIBIANS*, and within that section might be subheadings for *Frogs*, *Salamanders*, and *Newts*. Readers should always pay close attention to headings and subheadings, because they prime the brain for the information that is about to be delivered, and because they make it easy to go back and find particular details in a long text.

Describe the use of italics in a text.

Describe some strategies for distinguishing between fact and opinion.

Discuss the identification of an author's biases and stereotypes.

Describe how an author may appeal to the reader's cmotion.

Describe the logical fallacy known as the false analogy.

Describe the logical fallacy known as circular reasoning.

Readers must always be conscious of the distinction between fact and opinion. A fact can be subjected to analysis and can be either proved or disproved. An opinion, on the other hand, is the author's personal feeling, which may not be alterable by research, evidence, or argument. If the author writes that the distance from New York to Boston is about two hundred miles, he is stating a fact. But if he writes that New York is too crowded, then he is giving an opinion because there is no objective standard for overpopulation. An opinion may be indicated by words like *believe*, *think*, or *feel*. Also, an opinion may be supported by facts: for instance, the author might give the population density of New York as a reason for why it is overcrowded. An opinion supported by fact tends to be more convincing. When authors support their opinions with other opinions, the reader is unlikely to be moved.

Italics, like bold text and underlines, are used to emphasize important words, phrases, and sentences in a text. However, italics have other uses as well. A word is placed in italics when it is being discussed as a word: that is, when it is being defined or its use in a sentence is being described. For instance, it is appropriate to use italics when saying that *esoteric* is an unusual adjective. Italics are also used for long or large works, like books, magazines, long operas, and epic poems. Shorter works are typically placed within quotation marks. A reader should note how an author uses italics, as this is a marker of style and tone. Some authors use them frequently, creating a tone of high emotion, while others are more restrained in their use, suggesting calm and reason.

Authors will sometimes appeal to the reader's emotion in an attempt to persuade or to distract the reader from the weakness of his argument. For instance, the author may try to inspire the pity of the reader by delivering a heart-rending story. An author also might use the bandwagon approach, in which he suggests that his opinion is correct because it is held by a majority of people. Some authors resort delivering insults and harsh words against an opponent in an attempt to distract. In advertising, a common appeal is the testimonial, in which a famous person endorses a product. Of course, the fact that a celebrity likes something should not really mean anything to the reader. These and other emotional appeals are usually evidence of poor reasoning and a weak argument.

Every author has a point of view, but when an author ignores reasonable counterarguments or distorts opposing viewpoints, he is demonstrating a bias. A bias is evident whenever the author is unfair or inaccurate in his presentation. Bias may be intentional or unintentional, but it should always alert the reader to be skeptical of the argument being made. It should be noted that a biased author may still be correct. However, the author will be correct in spite of her bias, not because of it. A stereotype is like a bias, except that it is specifically applied to a group or place. Stereotyping is considered to be particularly abhorrent because it promotes negative generalizations about people. Many people are familiar with some of the hateful stereotypes of certain ethnic, religious, and cultural groups. Readers should be very wary of authors who stereotype. These faulty assumptions typically reveal the author's ignorance and lack of curiosity.

Circular reasoning is one of the more difficult logical fallacies to identify because it is typically hidden behind dense language and complicated sentences. Reasoning is described as circular when it offers no support for assertions other than restating them in different words. Put another way, a circular argument refers to itself as evidence of truth. A simple example of circular argument is when a person uses a word to define itself, such as saying *Niceness is the state of being nice*. If the reader does not know what *nice* means, then this definition will not be very useful. In a text, circular reasoning is usually more complex. For instance, an author might say *Poverty is a problem for society because it creates trouble for people throughout the community*. It is redundant to say that poverty is a problem because it creates trouble. When an author engages in circular reasoning, it is often because he or she has not fully thought out the argument or cannot come up with any legitimate justifications.

A logical fallacy is a failure of reasoning. As a reader, it is important to recognize logical fallacies, because they diminish the value of the author's message. The four most common logical fallacies in writing are the false analogy, circular reasoning, false dichotomy, and overgeneralization. In a false analogy, the author suggests that two things are similar, when in fact they are different. This fallacy is often committed when the author is attempting to convince the reader that something unknown is like something relatively familiar. The author takes advantage of the reader's ignorance to make this false comparison. One example might be the following statement: *Failing to tip a waitress is like stealing money out of somebody's wallet*. Of course, failing to tip is very rude, especially when the service has been good, but people are not arrested for failing to tip as they would be for stealing money from a wallet. To compare stingy diners with thieves is a false analogy.

Describe the logical fallacy known as false dichotomy.

Describe the logical fallacy known as overgeneralization.

Discuss the process of identifying the logical conclusion given a reading selection.

Compare and contrast topics and main ideas.

Discuss the identification and evaluation of supporting details.

Discuss the identification and evaluation of themes.

Overgeneralization is a logical fallacy in which the author makes a claim that is so broad it cannot be proved or disproved. In most cases, overgeneralization occurs when the author wants to create an illusion of authority or when he is using sensational language to sway the opinion of the reader. For instance, in the sentence *Everybody knows that she is a terrible teacher*, the author makes an assumption that cannot really be believed. This kind of statement is made when the author wants to create the illusion of consensus when none actually exists. It may be that most people have a negative view of the teacher, but to say that *everybody* feels that way is an exaggeration. When a reader spots overgeneralization, she should become skeptical about the argument that is being made because an author will often try to hide a weak or unsupported assertion behind authoritative language.

One of the most common logical fallacies is the false dichotomy, in which the author creates an artificial sense that there are only two possible alternatives in a situation. This fallacy is common when the author has an agenda and wants to give the impression that his view is the only sensible one. A false dichotomy has the effect of limiting the reader's options and imagination. An example of a false dichotomy is the statement *You need to go to the party with me, otherwise you'll just be bored at home*. The speaker suggests that the only other possibility besides being at the party is being bored at home. This is not true, as it is perfectly possible to be entertained at home, or even to go somewhere other than the party. Readers should always be wary of the false dichotomy: when an author limits alternatives, it is always wise to ask whether he is being valid.

One of the most important skills in reading comprehension is the identification of topics and main ideas. There is a subtle difference between these two features. The *topic* is the subject of a text, or what the text is about. The *main idea*, on the other hand, is the most important point being made by the author. The topic is usually expressed in few words, while the main idea often needs a full sentence to be completely defined. As an example, a short passage might have the topic of *penguins* and the main idea *Penguins are different from other birds in many ways*. In most nonfiction writing, the topic and the main idea will be stated directly, often in a sentence at the very beginning or end of the text. However, there are cases in which the reader must figure out an unstated topic or main idea. One way to approach this process is to read every sentence of the text, and try to come up with an overarching idea that is supported by each of those sentences.

Identifying a logical conclusion is much like making an inference: it requires the reader to combine the information given by the text with what he already knows to make a supportable assertion. If a passage is written well, then the conclusion should be obvious even when it is unstated. If the author intends the reader to draw a certain conclusion, then all of his argumentation and detail should be leading toward it. One way to approach the task of drawing conclusions is to make brief notes of all the points made by the author. When these are arranged on paper, they may clarify the logical conclusion. Another way to approach conclusions is to consider whether the reasoning of the author raises any pertinent questions. Sometimes it will be possible to draw several conclusions from a passage, and, on occasion, these will be conclusions that were never imagined by the author. It is essential, however, that these conclusions be supported directly by the text.

Themes are seldom expressed directly in a text, so they can be difficult to identify. A theme is an issue, an idea, or a question raised by the text. For instance, a theme of William Shakespeare's *Hamlet* is indecision, as the title character explores his own psyche and the results of his failure to make bold choices. A great work of literature may have many themes, and the reader is justified in identifying any for which he or she can find support. One common characteristic of themes is that they raise more questions than they answer. In a good piece of fiction, the author is not always trying to convince the reader, but may instead be trying to elevate the reader's perspective and encourage him to consider the themes more deeply. When reading, one can identify themes by constantly asking what general issues the text is addressing. A good way to evaluate an author's approach to a theme is to begin reading with a question in mind (for example, how does this text approach the theme of love?) and then look for evidence in the text that addresses that question.

Supporting details provide evidence and backing for the main point. All texts contain details, but they are only classified as supporting details when they serve to reinforce some larger point. Supporting details are most commonly found in informative and persuasive texts. In some cases, they will be clearly indicated with words like *for example* or *for instance*, or they will be enumerated with words like *first*, *second*, and *last*. However, these special words are not a requirement. As a reader, it is important to consider whether the author's supporting details really back up his or her main point. Supporting details can be factual and correct but still not relevant to the author's point. Conversely, supporting details can seem pertinent but be ineffective because they are based on opinion or assertions that cannot be proven.

Discuss the identification of the author's intent to persuade.

Discuss the identification of the author's intent to inform.

Discuss the identification of the author's intent to entertain.

Discuss the identification of the author's intent to express feelings.

Discuss the use of prior knowledge to make predictions about a piece of literature.

Describe the process of making inferences from a text.

An informative text is written to educate and enlighten the reader. Informative texts are almost always nonfiction, and are rarely structured as a story. The intention of an informative text is to deliver information in the most comprehensible way possible, so the structure of the text is likely to be very clear. In an informative text, the thesis statement is often in the first sentence. The author may use some colorful language, but is likely to put more emphasis on clarity and precision. Informative essays do not typically appeal to the emotions. They often contain facts and figures, and rarely include the opinion of the author. Sometimes a persuasive essay can resemble an informative essay, especially if the author maintains an even tone and presents his or her views as if they were established fact.

In a persuasive essay, the author is attempting to change the reader's mind or convince him of something he did not believe previously. There are several identifying characteristics of persuasive writing. One is opinion presented as fact. When an author attempts to persuade the reader, he often presents his or her opinions as if they were fact. A reader must be on guard for statements that sound factual but which cannot be subjected to research, observation, or experiment. Another characteristic of persuasive writing is emotional language. An author will often try to play on the reader's emotion by appealing to his sympathy or sense of morality. When an author uses colorful or evocative language with the intent of arousing the reader's passions, it is likely that he is attempting to persuade. Finally, in many cases a persuasive text will give an unfair explanation of opposing positions, if these positions are mentioned at all.

When an author intends to express feelings, she may use colorful and evocative language. An author may write emotionally for any number of reasons. Sometimes, the author will do so because she is describing a personal situation of great pain or happiness. Sometimes an author is attempting to persuade the reader and so will use emotion to stir up the passions. It can be easy to identify this kind of expression when the writer uses phrases like *I felt* and *I sense*. However, sometimes the author will simply describe feelings without introducing them. A reader should learn to recognize when an author is expressing emotion, and should not become overwhelmed by sympathy or passion. A reader should maintain some detachment so that he can evaluate the strength of the author's argument or the quality of the writing.

The success or failure of an author's intent to entertain is determined by those who read the author's work. Entertaining texts may be either fiction or nonfiction, and they may describe real or imagined people, places, and events. Entertaining texts are often narratives, or stories. A text that is written to entertain is likely to contain colorful language that engages the imagination and the emotions. Such writing often features a great deal of figurative language, which typically enlivens its subject matter with images and analogies. Though an entertaining text is not usually written to persuade or inform, it may accomplish both of these tasks. An entertaining text may appeal to the reader's emotions and cause him or her to think differently about a particular subject. In any case, entertaining texts tend to showcase the personality of the author more so than do other types of writing.

A text often makes claims and suggests ideas without stating them directly. An inference is a piece of information that is implied but not written outright by the author. For instance, consider the following sentence: *Mark made more money that week than he had in the previous year*. From this sentence, the reader can infer that Mark either has not made much money in the previous year or made a great deal of money that week. Often, a reader can use information he or she already knows to make inferences. Take as an example the sentence *When his coffee arrived, he looked around the table for the silver cup*. Many people know that cream is typically served in a silver cup, so using their own base of knowledge they can infer that the subject of this sentence takes his coffee with cream. Making inferences requires concentration, attention, and practice.

A prediction is a guess about what will happen next. Readers are constantly making predictions based on what they have read and what they already know. Making predictions is an important part of being an active reader. Consider the following sentence: *Staring at the computer screen in shock, Kim blindly reached over for the brimming glass of water on the shelf to her side*. The sentence suggests that Kim is agitated and that she is not looking at the glass she is going to pick up, so a reader might predict that she is going to knock the glass over. Of course, not every prediction will be accurate: perhaps Kim will pick the glass up cleanly. Nevertheless, the author has certainly created the expectation that the water might be spilled. Predictions are always subject to revision as the reader acquires more information.

Describe the problem-solution text structure.

Describe a descriptive text.

Describe how a sequence is described in writing.

Describe how an author compares and contrasts.

Describe how an author demonstrates cause and effect.

Discuss strategies for identifying an author's position.

In a sense, almost all writing is descriptive, insofar as it seeks to describe events, ideas, or people to the reader. Some texts, however, are primarily concerned with description. A descriptive text focuses on a particular subject, and attempts to depict it in a way that will be clear to the reader. Descriptive texts contain many adjectives and adverbs, words that give shades of meaning and create a more detailed mental picture for the reader. A descriptive text fails when it is unclear or vague to the reader. On the other hand, however, a descriptive text that compiles too much detail can be boring and overwhelming to the reader. A descriptive text will certainly be informative, and it may be persuasive and entertaining as well. Descriptive writing is a challenge for the author, but when it is done well, it can be fun to read.

Some nonfiction texts are organized to present a problem followed by a solution. In this type of text, it is common for the problem to be explained before the solution is offered. In some cases, as when the problem is well known, the solution may be briefly introduced at the beginning. Other times, the entire passage will focus on the solution, and the problem will be referenced only occasionally. This is common when the author can assume that the reading audience is already familiar with the problem. Some texts will outline multiple solutions to a problem, leaving the reader to choose among them. If the author has an interest or an allegiance to one solution, he may fail to mention or may describe inaccurately some of the other solutions. Readers should be careful of the author's agenda when reading a problem-solution text. Only by understanding the author's point of view and interests can one develop a proper judgment of the proposed solution.

When an author describes the ways in which two things are alike, he or she is comparing them. When the author describes the ways in which two things are different, he or she is contrasting them. The "compare and contrast" essay is one of the most common forms in nonfiction. It is often signaled with certain words: a comparison may be indicated with such words as *both*, *same*, *like*, *too*, and *as well*; while a contrast may be indicated by words like *but*, *however*, *on the other hand*, *instead*, and *yet*. Of course, comparisons and contrasts may be implicit without using any such signaling language. A single sentence may both compare and contrast. Consider the sentence *Brian and Sheila love ice cream, but Brian prefers vanilla and Sheila prefers strawberry*. In one sentence, the author has described both a similarity (love of ice cream) and a difference (favorite flavor).

A reader must be able to identify a text's sequence, or the order in which things happen. Often, and especially when the sequence is very important to the author, it is indicated with signal words like *first*, *then*, *next*, and *last*. However, sometimes a sequence is merely implied and must be noted by the reader. Consider the sentence *He walked in the front door and switched on the hall lamp*. Clearly, the man did not turn the lamp on before he walked in the door, so the implied sequence is that he first walked in the door and then turned on the lamp. Texts do not always proceed in an orderly sequence from first to last: sometimes, they begin at the end and then start over at the beginning. As a reader, it can be useful to make brief notes to clarify the sequence.

In order to be an effective reader, one must pay attention to the author's position and purpose. Even those texts that seem objective and impartial, like textbooks, have some sort of position and bias. Readers need to take these positions into account when considering the author's message. When an author uses emotional language or clearly favors one side of an argument, his position is clear. However, the author's position may be evident not only in what he writes, but in what he doesn't write. For this reason, it is sometimes necessary to review some other texts on the same topic in order to develop a view of the author's position. If this is not possible, then it may be useful to acquire a little background personal information about the author. When the only source of information is the text, however, the reader should look for language and argumentation that seems to indicate a particular stance on the subject.

One of the most common text structures is cause and effect. A cause is an act or event that makes something happen, and an effect is the thing that happens as a result of that cause. A cause-and-effect relationship is not always explicit, but there are some words in English that signal causality. These words include *since*, *because*, and *as a result*. As an example, consider the sentence *Because the sky was clear, Ron did not bring an umbrella*. The cause is the clear sky, and the effect is that Ron did not bring an umbrella. Sometimes the cause-and-effect relationship will not be clearly noted. For instance, the sentence *He was late and missed the meeting* does not contain any signaling words, but it still contains a cause (he was late) and an effect (he missed the meeting). It is possible for a single cause to have multiple effects, or for a single effect to have multiple causes. Also, an effect can in turn be the cause of another effect in what is known as a cause-and-effect chain.

Discuss issues related to identifying an author's purpose.

Describe some strategies for identifying an author's purpose.

Describe the characteristics of a narrative passage.

Describe the characteristics of an expository passage.

Describe the characteristics of a technical passage.

Describe the characteristics of a persuasive passage.

An author's purpose is often evident in the organization of the text. For instance, if the text has headings and subheadings, if key terms are in bold, and if the author makes his main idea clear from the beginning, then the likely purpose of the text is to inform. If the author begins by making a claim and then makes various arguments to support that claim, the purpose is probably to persuade. If the author is telling a story, or is more interested in holding the attention of the reader than in making a particular point or delivering information, then his purpose is most likely to entertain. As a reader, it is best to judge an author on how well he accomplishes his purpose. In other words, it is not entirely fair to complain that a textbook is boring: if the text is clear and easy to understand, then the author has done his job. Similarly, a storyteller should not be judged too harshly for getting some facts wrong, so long as he is able to give pleasure to the reader.

Identifying the purpose of an author is usually easier than identifying her position. In most cases, the author has no interest in hiding his or her purpose. A text that is meant to entertain, for instance, should be obviously written to please the reader. Most narratives, or stories, are written to entertain, though they may also inform or persuade. Informative texts are easy to identify as well. The most difficult purpose of a text to identify is persuasion because the author has an interest in making this purpose hard to detect. When a person knows that the author is trying to convince him, he is automatically more wary and skeptical of the argument. For this reason, persuasive texts often try to establish an entertaining tone, hoping to amuse the reader into agreement, or an informative tone, hoping to create an appearance of authority and objectivity.

An expository passage aims to inform and enlighten the reader. It is nonfiction and usually centers around a simple, easily defined topic. Since the goal of exposition is to teach, such a passage should be as clear as possible. It is common for an expository passage to contain helpful organizing words, like *first*, *next*, *for example*, and *therefore*. These words keep the reader oriented in the text. Although expository passages do not need to feature colorful language and artful writing, they are often more effective when they do. For a reader, the challenge of expository passages is to maintain steady attention. Expository passages are not always about subjects in which a reader will naturally be interested, and the writer is often more concerned with clarity and comprehensibility than with engaging the reader. For this reason, expository passages can be dull. Making notes is a good way to maintain focus when reading an expository passage.

A narrative passage is a story. Narratives can be either fiction or nonfiction, but there are a few elements that a text must have in order to be classified as a narrative. To begin with, the text must have a plot. That is, it must describe a series of events. If it is a good narrative, these events will be interesting and emotionally engaging to the reader. A narrative also has characters. These could be people, animals, or even inanimate objects, so long as they participate in the plot. A narrative passage often contains figurative language, which is meant to stimulate the imagination of the reader by making comparisons and observations. A metaphor, which is a description of one thing in terms of another, is a common piece of figurative language. *The moon was a frosty snowball* is an example of a metaphor: it is untrue in the literal sense, but it suggests a certain mood for the reader. Narratives often proceed in a clear sequence, but they do not need to do so.

A persuasive passage is meant to change the reader's mind or lead her into agreement with the author. The persuasive intent may be obvious or it may be quite difficult to discern. In some cases, a persuasive passage will be indistinguishable from an informative passage: it will make an assertion and offer supporting details. However, a persuasive passage is more likely to make claims based on opinion and to appeal to the reader's emotions. Persuasive passages may not describe alternate positions and, when they do, they often display significant bias. It may be clear that a persuasive passage is giving the author's viewpoint or the passage may adopt a seemingly objective tone. A persuasive passage is successful if it can make a convincing argument and win the trust of the reader.

A technical passage is written to describe a complex object or process. Technical writing is common in medical and technological fields, in which complicated mathematical, scientific, and engineering ideas need to be explained simply and clearly. To ease comprehension, a technical passage usually proceeds in a very logical order. Technical passages often have clear headings and subheadings which are used to keep the reader oriented in the text. It is also common for these passages to break sections up with numbers or letters. Many technical passages look more like an outline than a piece of prose. The amount of difficult vocabulary or field-specific jargon will vary depending on the intended audience. As much as possible, technical passages try to avoid language that the reader will have to research in order to understand the message, though this is not always possible

Discuss the influences of the historical context on a literary work.

Discuss drawing conclusions.

Discuss the importance of answering the related questions only from the reading.

Discuss determining the topic of the reading passage.

Discuss making comparisons and contrasts in the reading passage.

Discuss contextual clues.

When asked for a *conclusion* that may be drawn, look for critical "hedge" phrases, such as likely, may, can, will often, sometimes, etc, often, almost, mostly, usually, generally, rarely, sometimes.

Test writers insert these hedge phrases to cover every possibility. An answer can be wrong simply because it leaves no room for exception. Extreme positive or negative answers (such as always, never, etc.) are usually not correct.

Historical context has a profound influence on literature: the events, knowledge base, and assumptions of an author's time color every aspect of his or her work. Sometimes, authors hold opinions and use language that would be considered inappropriate or immoral in a modern setting but that was acceptable in the author's time. As a reader, one should consider how the historical context influenced a work and also how today's opinions and ideas shape the way modern readers read the works of the past. For instance, in most societies of the past, women were treated as second-class citizens. An author who wrote in 18th-century England might sound sexist to modern readers, even if that author was relatively feminist in his time. Readers should not have to excuse the faulty assumptions and prejudices of the past, but they should appreciate that a person's thoughts and words are, in part, a result of the time and culture in which they live or lived, and it is perhaps unfair to expect writers to avoid all of the errors of their times.

Your first task when you begin reading is to answer the question "What is the topic of the selection?" This can best be answered by quickly *skimming* the passage for the general idea, stopping to read only the first sentence of each paragraph. A paragraph's first sentence is usually the main topic sentence; it gives you a summary of the content of the paragraph.

When testing, the reader should not use any outside knowledge that is not gathered from the reading passage to answer the related questions unless specifically instructed to do so. Correct answers can be derived straight from the reading passage.

Look for contextual clues. When testing, an answer can be *right* but not *correct*. The contextual clues will help you find the answer that is *most right* and is correct. Understand the context in which a phrase is stated. When asked for the implied meaning of a statement made in the passage, immediately go find the statement and read the context in which it was made. Also, look for an answer choice that has a similar phrase to the statement in question.

The author will often present *comparisons* and *contrasts* in the reading passage. These are often couples with signal words, such as: more, most, less, least, but, or, instead, then-now, and before-after.

Discuss making predictions of the future.

Explain what an analogy is and discuss some common relationships used in analogies.

Discuss the difference between paraphrasing and summarizing.

Describe the organizational structures of *cause and effect* and *chronological order*.

Explain what is meant by the term *text evidence* and indicate how it can be used to draw a conclusion from a story.

Explain how the author's point of view can influence the plot of a story.

An analogy is a comparison of two things. The words in the analogy are connected by a certain (sometimes undetermined) relationship. Look at this analogy: moo is to cow as quack is to duck. This analogy compares the sound that a cow makes with the sound that a duck makes. Even if the word 'quack' was not given, one could figure out it is the correct word to complete the analogy based on the relationship between the words 'moo' and 'cow'. Some common relationships for analogies include synonyms, antonyms, part to whole, definition, and actor to action.

When testing, to respond to questions requiring future predictions, base your answers on evidence of past or present behavior.

An author should organize information logically so the reader can follow it and locate information within the text. Two common organizational structures are *cause and effect* and *chronological order*. In *cause and effect*, an author presents one thing that makes something else happen. For example, if one were to go to bed very late, they would be tired. The cause is going to bed late, with the effect of being tired the next day. When using *chronological order*, the author presents information in the order that it happened. For example, biographies are written in chronological order; the subject's birth and childhood are presented first, followed by their adult life, and lastly by the events leading up to the person's death.

Paraphrasing and summarizing are two methods one can use to help them understand what they read. When paraphrasing, one puts what they have read into their own words, rephrasing what the author has written to make it their own, to "translate" all of what the author says to their own words, including as many details as they can. When summarizing, on the other hand, one does not include many details, but rather simply the main idea of the text. Often times, a summary can be done in just one or two sentences, boiling down the author's words into just main idea.

The author will always have a point of view about a story before they draw up a plot line. The author will know what events they want to take place, how they want the characters to interact, and how the story will resolve. An author will also have an opinion on the topic, or series of events, which is presented in the story, based on their own prior experience and beliefs.
A story can be taken in whatever direction the author wishes. A story will often make sense based on societal norms, but the author can purposely choose to go against these norms to shock the reader. For example, if an author wrote a story about a man who enjoyed living in the bayous of Louisiana, the audience would not expect the character to promptly move to Alaska. Sometimes an author will put a twist in a story just to surprise the reader.

The term *text evidence* refers to information that supports a main point or points in a story. Information used as *text evidence* is precise, descriptive, and factual. A main point is often followed by supporting details that provide evidence to back-up a claim. For example, a story may include the claim that winter occurs during opposite months in the Northern and Southern hemispheres. *Text evidence* based on this claim may include countries where winter occurs in opposite months, along with reasons that winter occurs at different times of the year in separate hemispheres (due to the tilt of the Earth as it rotates around the sun).

Describe the difference between a main idea and a supporting detail.

Describe ways to distinguish between *fact* and *opinion* in a text.

Describe how a reader can use text to defend his or her own response or interpretation.

Explain what point of view is and describe different points of view that authors use.

Discuss the use of transitional words and phrases.

Describe the process of making claims in a persuasive essay.

A *fact* is based on information that is presented to the reader from reliable sources. Facts are accurate until proven otherwise. An *opinion* is what the author thinks about a given topic. An opinion is not common knowledge or proven by expert sources, but it is information that the author believes and wants the reader to consider. To distinguish between fact and opinion, a reader needs to look at the type of source that is presenting information, what information backs-up a claim, and whether or not the author may be motivated to have a certain point of view on a given topic. For example, if a panel of scientists has conducted multiple studies on the effectiveness of taking a certain vitamin, the results are more likely to be factual than if a company selling a vitamin claims that taking the vitamin can produce positive effects. The company is motivated to sell its product, while the scientists are using the scientific method to prove a theory. If the author uses words such as "I think...", the statement is an opinion.

A main idea is the overall premise of a story, or what the author wants the reader to know about their topic in general. In order to show that a main idea is correct, or valid, the author needs to add details that prove their point. Sentences that help to prove the point of the story are called supporting details.

The main idea is often found near the beginning of a story so that the reader knows what the rest of the story will be about. Supporting details need to follow the main idea, since there is nothing to support without a main concept to adhere to! An example of a main idea is: "Giraffes live in the Serengeti of Africa." A supporting detail about giraffes could be: "A giraffe uses its long neck to reach twigs and leaves on trees." The main idea gives the general idea that the text is about giraffes. The supporting detail gives a specific fact about how the giraffes eat.

The point of view of a text is the perspective from which it is told. Every literary text has a narrator or person who tells the story. The two main points of view that authors use are first person and third person. If a narrator is also the main character, or protagonist, the text is written in first-person point of view. The author writes with the word *I*. Third-person point of view is probably the most common point of view that authors use. Using third person, authors refer to each character using the words *he* or *she*. In third-person omniscient, the narrator is not a character in the story and tells the story of all of the characters at the same time.

Readers can interpret text and respond to it in a number of ways. Using textual support helps defend your response or interpretation because it roots your thinking in the text. You are interpreting based on information in the text and not simply your own ideas. When crafting a response, look for important quotes and details from the text to help bolster your argument. If you are writing about a character's personality trait, for example, use details from the text to show that the character acted in such a way. You can also include statistics and facts from a nonfiction text to strengthen your response. For example, instead of writing, "A lot of people use cell phones," use statistics to provide the exact number. This strengthens your argument because it is more precise.

A persuasive essay will likely focus on one central argument, but it may make many smaller claims along the way. These are subordinate arguments with which the reader must agree if he or she is going to agree with the central argument. The central argument will only be as strong as the subordinate claims. These claims should be rooted in fact and observation, rather than subjective judgment. The best persuasive essays provide enough supporting detail to justify claims without overwhelming the reader. Remember that a fact must be susceptible to independent verification: that is, it must be something the reader could confirm. Also, statistics are only effective when they take into account possible objections. For instance, a statistic on the number of foreclosed houses would only be useful if it was taken over a defined interval and in a defined area. Most readers are wary of statistics because they are so often misleading. If possible, a persuasive essay should always include references so that the reader can obtain more information. Of course, this means that the writer's accuracy and fairness may be judged by the inquiring reader.

A good writer will use transitional words and phrases to guide the reader through the text. You are no doubt familiar with the common transitions, though you may never have considered how they operate. Some transitional phrases (*after, before, during, in the middle of*) give information about time. Some indicate that an example is about to be given (*for example, in fact, for instance*). Writers use them to compare (*also, likewise*) and contrast (*however, but, yet*). Transitional words and phrases can suggest addition (*and, also, furthermore, moreover*) and logical relationships (*if, then, therefore, as a result, since*). Finally, transitional words and phrases can demarcate the steps in a process (*first, second, last*). Authors incorporate transitional words and phrases where they will orient the reader and illuminate the structure of their composition.

Discuss the use of emotional appeals in a persuasive essay.

Identify the elements that should be included in a summary of a text.

Explain how to evaluate the credibility of a text.

Discuss how to use elements of a text to support or defend one's response to it.

Explain how an author's motivations may impact the credibility of a text.

Discuss how a reader can recognize a logical fallacy in an argument.

A summary is an abbreviated version of a text, including only the main idea and key supporting details. A summary of an article, for example, can be a one paragraph description of the main idea. All details not necessary to understand the main idea of the article should not be included in the summary. A summary is an overview of the author's text and should be broad and short.

Opinions are formed by emotion as well as reason, and persuasive writers often appeal to the feelings of the reader. Although readers may be skeptical of this technique, it is often used in a proper and ethical manner. For instance, there are many subjects that have an obvious emotional component, and therefore cannot be completely treated without an appeal to the emotions. Consider an article on drunk driving: it makes sense to include some specific examples that will alarm or sadden the reader. After all, drunk driving often has serious and tragic consequences. Emotional appeals are not appropriate, however, when they attempt to mislead the reader. For instance, in political advertisements it is common to emphasize the patriotism of the preferred candidate, because this will encourage the audience to link their own positive feelings about the country with their opinion of the candidate. However, these ads often imply that the other candidate is unpatriotic, which in most cases is far from the truth. Another common and improper emotional appeal is the use of loaded language, as for instance referring to an avidly religious person as a "fanatic" or a passionate environmentalist as a "tree hugger." These terms introduce an emotional component that detracts from the argument.

When writing a response to a text, it is important to use elements of the text to support your assertion or defend your position. Using supporting evidence from the text strengthens the argument because the reader can see how in depth the writer read the original piece and based their response on the details and facts within that text. Elements of text that can be used in a response include: facts, details, statistics, and direct quotations from the text. When writing a response, one must make sure they indicate which information comes from the original text and then base their discussion, argument, or defense around this information.

When evaluating the credibility of a text, the reader must look at the author of the text. If the author has a specific agenda (i.e., a political lobbyist), that text is going to be biased in a particular direction. The author's motivations for writing the text play a critical role in determining its credibility.
The extent of the author's knowledge of the topic and their motivation must be evaluated when assessing the credibility of a text. For example, reports written about the Ozone layer by an environmental scientist and a hairdresser will have a different level of credibility.

A logical fallacy occurs when an author attempts to use common errors in reasoning to persuade his readers. Two types of logical fallacies are "slippery slope" and "hasty generalizations." In a "slippery slope" fallacy, the author asserts a certain effect is certain when a specific cause exists, even though this may not be true. (For example, "If you study hard, you will ace the test.") "Hasty generalization" fallacies drawing a conclusion too early without finishing analyzing the details of the argument. Writers of persuasive texts often use these techniques because they are very effective. In order to identify logical fallacies, readers need to read carefully and ask questions as they read. Thinking critically means not taking everything at face value. Readers need to critically evaluate an author's argument to make sure that the logic used is sound.

A text is credible, or believable, when the author is both knowledgeable and objective. When evaluating the credibility of a text, it is important to look at the author of the text. The author's motives should be for the dissemination of information. The purpose of the text should be to inform or describe, not to persuade. When an author writes a persuasive text, he has the motivation that the reader will do what they want. If a text is being written by a author with a specific agenda (i.e., a political lobbyist), that text is going to be biased in a particular direction. The author's motivations for writing the text play a critical role in determining the credibility of the text and must be evaluated when assessing that credibility.

Describe the identification of cause-and-effect relationships in a text.

Describe how an author may use cause-and-effect relationships in a persuasive essay.

Discuss finding the order of events in a passage with an unorthodox structure.

Discuss the analysis of relationships between ideas in opposition.

Discuss the identification of the order of events or steps described in written material.

Discuss the analysis of relationships between similar ideas.

Persuasive essays, in which an author tries to make a convincing argument and change the reader's mind, usually include cause-and-effect relationships. However, these relationships should not always be taken at face value. An author frequently will assume a cause or take an effect for granted. To read a persuasive essay effectively, one needs to judge the cause-and-effect relationships the author is presenting. For instance, imagine an author wrote the following: "The parking deck has been unprofitable because people would prefer to ride their bikes." The relationship is clear: the cause is that people prefer to ride their bikes, and the effect is that the parking deck has been unprofitable. However, a reader should consider whether this argument is conclusive. Perhaps there are other reasons for the failure of the parking deck: a down economy, excessive fees, etc. Too often, authors present causal relationships as if they are fact rather than opinion. Readers should be on the alert for these dubious claims.

It can be tricky to identify the cause-and-effect relationships in a text, but there are a few ways to approach this task. To begin with, these relationships are often signaled with certain terms. When an author uses words like *because*, *since*, *in order*, and *so*, she is likely describing a cause-and-effect relationship. Consider the sentence, "He called her because he needed the homework." This is a simple causal relationship, in which the cause was his need for the homework and the effect was his phone call. Not all cause-and-effect relationships are marked in this way, however. Consider the sentences, "He called her. He needed the homework." When the cause-and-effect relationship is not indicated with a keyword, it can be discovered by asking why something happened. He called her: why? The answer is in the next sentence: He needed the homework.

The analysis of opposing ideas is known as contrast. Contrast is often marred by the author's obvious partiality to one of the ideas. A discerning reader will be put off by an author who does not engage in a fair fight. In an analysis of opposing ideas, both ideas should be presented in their clearest and most reasonable terms. If the author does prefer a side, he should avoid indicating this preference with pejorative language. An analysis of opposing ideas should proceed through the major differences point by point, with a full explanation of each side's view. For instance, in an analysis of capitalism and communism, it would be important to outline each side's view on labor, markets, prices, personal responsibility, etc. It would be less effective to describe the theory of communism and then explain how capitalism has thrived in the West. An analysis of opposing views should present each side in the same manner.

Most texts place events in chronological or sequential order, mainly to avoid confusing the reader. However, some authors may employ an unorthodox structure to achieve a certain effect. For instance, many of the Greek epics begin *in medias res*, or "in the middle of things." The text begins with an account of a climactic moment, after which the author goes back to the beginning to describe how events led up to that climax. This technique is often found in mystery novels: a crime is committed and the detective must reconstruct the events that caused it. For the reader, it may be helpful to keep in mind the cause-and-effect relationships that shape the story. By definition, a cause must precede an effect. Therefore, an outline of the various causes and effects in a text will mimic the chronological sequence. Readers should remember that the order in which events are described in a text is not necessarily the order in which they occurred.

Many texts follow the compare-and-contrast model, in which the similarities and differences between two ideas or things are explored. Analysis of the similarities between ideas is called comparison. In order for a comparison to work, the author must place the ideas or things in an equivalent structure. That is, the author must present the ideas in the same way. Imagine an author wanted to show the similarities between cricket and baseball. The correct way to do so would be to summarize the equipment and rules for each game. It would be incorrect to summarize the equipment of cricket and then lay out the history of baseball, since this would make it impossible for the reader to see the similarities. It is perhaps too obvious to say that an analysis of similar ideas should emphasize the similarities. Of course, the author should take care to include any differences that must be mentioned. Often, these small differences will only reinforce the more general similarity.

Often, a reader will have to understand the sequence of events or steps in a process in order to understand a text. In many cases, the author will facilitate this process by using key words, like *first*, *second*, *third*, *then*, *next*, and *finally*. These words orient the reader in the text; they place events in order and establish a clear structure. However, a writer will not always outline the order of events so clearly, in part because it can be tedious to structure a passage "first...second...then..." and so on. The reader may have to do a little work. One way to approach this task is to continue asking the question "And then what?" If the text is a string of declarative sentences ("The battle raged. A white flag was waved. The peace treaty was signed."), a reader can discover the sequence of events simply by repeating this question.

Discuss the process of drawing conclusions from information stated within a passage.

Discuss the process of drawing conclusions from information implied within a passage.

Discuss the process of identifying an effective outline of information presented in a paragraph or message.

Discuss the process of identifying an effective summary of information presented in a paragraph or passage.

What is a slash used for in poetry?

What are some common uses of the comma?

Drawing conclusions from information implied within a passage requires confidence on the part of the reader. Implications are things the author does not state directly, but which can be assumed based on what the author does say. For instance, consider the following simple passage: "I stepped outside and opened my umbrella. By the time I got to work, the cuffs of my pants were soaked." The author never states that it is raining, but this fact is clearly implied. Conclusions based on implication must be well supported by the text. In order to draw a solid conclusion, a reader should have multiple pieces of evidence, or, if he only has one, must be assured that there is no other possible explanation than his conclusion. A good reader will be able to draw many conclusions from information implied by the text, which enriches the reading experience considerably.

A reader should always be drawing conclusions from the text, even if these conclusions are only provisional. It is always more comfortable to draw conclusions from information stated within a passage, rather than to draw them from mere implications. However, an author may provide some information and then describe a counterargument. The reader should be alert for direct statements that are subsequently rejected or weakened by the author. The reader should always read the entire passage before drawing conclusions. Many readers are trained to expect the author's conclusions at either the beginning or the end of the passage. However, many texts will not adhere to this format. The reader should be adept at outlining the information contained in the passage; an effective outline will reveal the structure of the passage, and will lead to solid conclusions.

Evaluating a summary of the information presented in a paragraph or message is similar to assessing an outline. To begin with, a summary should accurately define the main idea of the passage. Because it is a summary, it does not need to explain this main idea in exhaustive detail. However, a summary should continue by laying out the most important supporting details or arguments from the passage. All of the significant supporting details should be included, and none of the details included should be irrelevant or insignificant. Also, the summary should accurately report all of these details. Too often, the desire for brevity in a summary leads to the sacrifice of clarity or veracity. Summaries are often difficult to read, because they omit all of graceful language, digressions, and asides that distinguish great writing. However, if the summary is effective, it should contain much the same message as the original text.

To evaluate an outline, one must first assess the accuracy and relevance of the outline's title. The title must refer to the basic subject of the text, though it need not recapitulate the main idea. In most outlines, the main idea will be the first major section. An effective outline will have each major idea of the passage established as the head of a category. For instance, the most common outline format calls for the main ideas of the passage to be indicated with Roman numerals. In an effective outline of this kind, each of the main ideas will be represented by a Roman numeral and none of the Roman numerals will designate minor details or secondary ideas. Moreover, all supporting ideas and details should be placed in the appropriate place on the outline. An outline does not need to include every detail listed in the text, but it should feature all of those that are central to the argument or message. Each of these details should be listed under the appropriate main idea.

1. Commas may be used to separate the items in a sequence (three or more things). For example, "She went to the store, dropped off the clothes at the dry cleaners, and stopped by the post office."
2. Use a comma along with a conjunction (and, but, for, nor, yet, or, so) to connect two independent clauses. For example, "She wanted to go to the store, but she did not have a car."
3. Use a comma to set off introductory elements. For example, "Driving to the grocery store, she suddenly realized that she forgot her purse."
4. Use a comma to set off parenthetical elements. For example, "The Statue of Liberty, which stands in New York Harbor, was a gift to the United States."

A slash (/) is used to separate lines of poetry that are part of the text of a paper. An example would be this line of poetry: "What soft, cherubic creatures / these gentle women are / One would as soon assault a plush / or violate a star."

Describe a comma splice.

Describe a sentence fragment.

Describe an appositive.

What are some common uses of the semicolon?

Provide examples of conjunctive adverbs and transition words.

Discuss apostrophe uses.

Sentence fragments happen by treating a dependent clause or other incomplete thought as a complete sentence. This error can typically be corrected by combining it with another sentence to make a complete thought.

Incorrect: Because I forgot the exam was today.

Correct: I forgot the exam was today.

A comma splice is the use of a comma between two independent clauses. A comma splice can typically be corrected by changing the comma to a period and therefore making the two clauses into two separate sentences, by changing the comma to a semicolon, or by making one clause dependent by inserting a dependent marker word in front of it.

Incorrect: She eats an apple every day, it tastes delicious.

Correct: She eats an apple every day. It tastes delicious.

(or) She eats an apple every day; it tastes delicious.

(or) She eats an apple every day, and it tastes delicious.

(or) She eats an apple every day because it tastes delicious.

(or) Because it tastes delicious, she eats an apple every day.

1. Semicolons are used to join independent clauses that aren't joined by a coordinating conjunction. For example, "Susie has brown hair; Susie's brother has red hair."

2. Semicolons are used to join two independent clauses connected by a conjunctive adverb or a transition word. For example, "In Washington D.C., she visited the National Archives; however, she never made it to the Smithsonian Institute."

3. Semicolons are used to separate items in a sequence containing internal punctuation. For example, "Our evening activities are first, cook dinner; second, eat dinner; third, exercise."

An appositive is a word or phrase that restates or modifies an immediately preceding noun. An appositive is often useful as a context clue for determining or refining the meaning of the word or words to which it refers. For example, "My dad, whose name is James Brown, (appositive) is a lawyer.

1. Use an apostrophe for contractions. Example: has not – hasn't

2. Use an apostrophe to show possession with plural nouns ending in "s". Example: the boys' cars

Conjunctive adverbs include the following: also, besides, consequently, finally, furthermore, however, indeed, likewise, moreover, nevertheless, next, nonetheless, otherwise, similarly, specifically, then, therefore

Transition Words include the following: as a matter of fact, as a result, at the same time, for example, for instance, in addition, in conclusion, in fact, in the first place, on the other hand, to the contrary

Describe colon uses.

How is a dash used?

What are some common uses of quotation marks?

What are the uses of an ellipsis?

Describe the function of an adjective.

Describe the differences between an independent clause and a dependent clause. Also discuss the various types of dependent clauses.

Dashes are used ( ) before an explanatory list following a complete sentence (A dash is less formal than a colon.) For example, "The coach gave her an exercise schedule--run three miles every other day, lift weights three times a week, stretch morning and evening, and swim laps.
The stew calls for all of the following--lamb, pork, tomatoes, and onions.

1. Use a colon before an explanatory list following a complete sentence. For example, "The boy had an interest in one of the following: softball, soccer, football, or basketball.
2. Use a colon before an independent clause that follows and explains the previous sentence.
3. Use a colon before a quotation.
4. Patrick Henry once said: "Give me liberty or give me death."
5. Use a colon after the greeting in a formal letter.
Dear Mr. President:
Dear Madam:

1. Use an ellipsis to indicate that you deleted words from a quotation.
2. Use an ellipsis to omit a sentence within a quotation, use an ellipsis and a period (....).

1. Use double quotation marks(" ") to enclose direct quotes. Example – Nathan Hale said, "I only regret that I have but one life to lose for my country."
2. Use double quotation marks to enclose titles of chapters of books, newspaper & magazine articles, short stories, songs and poems.
3. Use single quotation marks (' ') to set off a quotation within a quotation. Example - Dr. Sherman said that "George Washington did not say 'I cannot tell a lie' although Americans enjoy believing that he did."

An *independent clause* is a group of words that contains a subject and verb and expresses a complete thought. An independent clause is a sentence.
A *dependent clause* is a group of words that contains a subject and verb but does not express a complete thought. A dependent clause cannot be a sentence. Dependent clauses can be a noun clause, adjective clause, or an adverb clause.
A *noun clause* can be a subject, a direct or indirect object, or an object of a preposition. Noun clauses can begin with wh- question words (what, which, when, where, who, whom) and question words like how, if, that.
An *adjective clause* modifies a noun or a pronoun. An adjective clause begins with who, whom, which, that, whose, when, where, why and follows the word it modifies.
An *adverb clause* modifies a verb, an adjective, another adverb, or a sentence. An adverb clause answers the question when? where? why? how? to what degree? and under what condition? An adverb clause begins with a subordinating conjunction, such as after, because, since, unless, etc.

An *adjective* modifies a noun, a pronoun, or another adjective by answering the following questions: What kind of? Which one? How many? How much?
Adjectives can appear in three places: before a noun, after a linking or sensory verb (be, feel, look, seem, smell, sound, etc.), and after a direct object as an objective complement.
Examples:
1. The United States is a wonderful place to live. (adjective is before a noun)
2. The baby seems happier after a nap. (adjective follows a linking verb)
3. The military has worked to keep us safe. (the adjective is an objective complement)
Nouns, pronouns, and participles sometimes act as adjectives.
Examples:
1. The student government elected a president. noun
2. This is a exciting time. present participle
3. We viewed the demolished building. past participle
4. This china is very old. demonstrative pronoun
5. Which movie did you see? interrogative pronoun
6. His haircut was hideous. possessive pronoun

Discuss equal comparison adjectives.

Discuss unequal comparison adjectives.

Describe adjective phrases.

Describe the function of an adverb.

Discuss adverb equal comparisons.

Discuss adverb phrases

Unequal comparisons:
Comparative: to compare two things use -er/more, less.
Superlative: to refer to the one in a group of three or more that is the outstanding example, use -est/most, least.
One-syllable adjectives use -er/est or less/least
Positive: new
Comparative: newer
Superlative: the newest
Two-syllable adjectives ending in 'y' use -er/est or less/least
Positive: hungry
Comparative: hungrier
Superlative: the hungriest
Two or more syllables use more/most; less/least
Positive: thrilling
Comparative: more thrilling
Superlative: the most thrilling
A few adjectives have irregular comparative and superlative forms.
Positive: bad
Comparative: worse than
Superlative: the worst

Equal comparisons - Use as...as to compare two persons, places, or things which are apparently the same.
Examples:
1. He is as short as I am.
2. Her cat is as fussy as his cat is.
3. Josh's swing is as old and rusty as mine is.
4. That little chair is as expensive as my big sofa.

An *adverb* modifies a verb, an adjective, or another adverb by answering such questions as how? how much? how long? when? and where? Adverbs also act as sentence modifiers.
1. He dressed handsomely. how?
2. She knows more than she thinks. how much?
3. He was gone a week. how long?
3. Last month they flew to Hawaii. when?
4. I went home. where?
5. Unfortunately, he revealed the story's surprise ending. sentence modifier
Other Parts of Speech as Adverbs - Nouns, prepositions and adjectives sometimes act as adverbs.
1. I'll see you Friday. noun when?
2. He came outside. preposition where?
3. My brother Fred runs slow. adjective how?
Adverbs Formed by Adding 'LY' to Adjectives - An adverb is often formed by adding an 'ly' to an adjective.

Adjective phrases are groups of words used as adjectives.
Participial phrases consist of a participle, its object, and any modifiers. Participles show tense and voice.
1. The boy shooting the ball is the team captain.
2. Having finished his homework, Jerry watched TV.
3. The most popular chocolate (being) eaten today is dark chocolate. (passive voice)
Infinitive phrases consist of to+verb, its object, and any modifiers. Infinitives show tense and voice.
1. The play to read for class is Romeo and Juliet.
2. Life is to be enjoyed. passive voice
Prepositional phrases consist of a preposition, its object, and any modifiers.
1. The dog with the spots is a Dalmatian.
2. The President lives in a mansion in Washington D.C.

Adverb phrases are groups of words used as adverbs.
Prepositional phrases consist of a preposition, its object, and any modifiers.
1. Jonah lived in a whale for a month. how long?
2. Jack and Jill walked to the store. where?
3. They got married after leaving town. when?
Infinitive phrases consist of to+verb, any object, and modifiers.
1. My grandfather left home to sail around the world. why?
2. It costs a lot of money to get a good education. clause modifier
Absolute phrases consist of a participle, its subject, and any modifiers. Absolute phrases modify the entire sentence.
The crowd being totally out of control, the police shot off tear gas.

Equal Comparisons - Use as...as to compare two similar actions.
1. Jane cooks as good as her mother does.
2. The faucet drips as slowly as molasses.
3. He never managed as successfully as his brother did.
4. Citizens are treated as well as non-citizens in Albania.

Describe the function of articles.

Discuss adverb unequal comparisons.

Describe subordinating conjunctions.

Describe coordinating and correlative conjunctions.

Describe the function of a noun.

Describe mass, collective, and abstract nouns.

Unequal Comparisons Adverbs can be used to compare and contrast dissimilar actions.
Comparative: to compare two actions, use -er/more, less.
Superlative: to refer to the one in a group of three or more that is the outstanding example of the action, use -est/most, least.
One-syllable adverbs use -er/est or less/least
Positive: late
Comparative: later
Superlative: the latest

Two & more syllables use more/most or less/least
Positive: carefully
Comparative: more carefully
Superlative: the most carefully
Irregular Adverbs
Positive: well
Comparative: better
Superlative: the best

Articles (an/an/the) come before a noun and provide important information. "A/an" are often identified as indefinite articles while "the" is identified as the definite article.
Use a/an with singular count nouns to introduce a singular count noun or to discuss all members of a category.
Omit article with plural count nouns and non-count nouns to indicate some, an indefinite amount; to discuss an abstract non-count noun; and to represent all members of a category.
Use "the" with count nouns and non-count nouns to indicate something that has already been mentioned; to indicate that reader and writer know the something which they refer to; to indicate a noun identified by an adjective phrase or adjective clause; to indicate one of a kind; in science, to represent all members of a category.

Conjunctions join words, phrases, and clauses, showing the relationship between them.
The categories of conjunctions are coordinating, correlative, and subordinating. Conjunctive adverbs or transition words are another type of conjunction.
Coordinating conjunctions join grammatically equal words, phrases, or clauses (two pronouns, two prepositional phrases, two independent clauses, etc.) The coordinating conjunctions are and, but, or, nor.
Correlative conjunctions are used in pairs to join two or more words, phrases, or clauses that are grammatically equal.
Examples:
both...and; not only...but also; either...or; whether...or; neither...nor

Subordinating conjunctions introduce adverbial clauses. They join a dependent adverb clause to an independent clause.
Cause: as, because, since
Comparison: more than, as...as
Conditional: even if, if, unless
Contrast: although, even though, though
Manner: as, as if, as though
Place: where, wherever
Purpose: in order that, so that
Result: so...that
Time: after, before, since, until, when

Mass nouns are concrete nouns that name things that cannot be separated into individual units--snow, sugar, water, air, toothpaste.
Collective nouns identify collections of different kinds of things: equipment, furniture, luggage, traffic. For example, furniture includes chairs, tables, sofas, etc.
Abstract nouns identify qualities, emotions, concepts. Abstract nouns name things that cannot be touched, seen, smelled, heard, or tasted--happiness, anger, love, liberty, equality, democracy. Abstract nouns are not introduced by "the" unless the noun is limited or described in some way--the liberty we cherish.

Nouns name things--persons, places, actions or ideas. Nouns are subjects, direct objects, indirect objects, objects of prepositions, predicate complements and predicate nouns. Nouns also show possession. Most nouns name things that can be counted-one potato, two potatoes, three potatoes. Most count nouns are concrete nouns. They name things that can be touched, seen, smelled, heard, tasted-table, movie, flower, song, candy bar. A/an are used with singular count nouns. "The" is used with both singular and plural count nouns.
Collective count nouns identify groups-family, team, herd, crowd, class. Although these nouns represent a group of individuals, they are understood as one unit and take a singular verb. When they represent two or more groups, they are plural. Most count nouns form the plural by adding "s" Example: toe-toes. Irregular count nouns form the plural in a variety of ways: count nouns ending in "s, sh, x, or z" add "es"; some count nouns change forms; some count nouns stay the same. Non-count nouns name things that can't be counted. Follow these rules. Never add "s" to a non-count noun; always use a singular verb; never use a/an with a non-count noun; never use many with a non-count noun.

Sentence Skills
© Mometrix Media - flashcardsecrets.com/accuplacer

Discuss comparing nouns.

Discuss noun phrases.

Sentence Skills
© Mometrix Media - flashcardsecrets.com/accuplacer

Sentence Skills
© Mometrix Media - flashcardsecrets.com/accuplacer

Describe the parts of speech.

Describe infinitive, participial, and prepositional phrases.

Sentence Skills
© Mometrix Media - flashcardsecrets.com/accuplacer

Sentence Skills
© Mometrix Media - flashcardsecrets.com/accuplacer

Describe the functions of pronouns, as well as personal pronouns, interrogative pronouns, and relative pronouns.

Describe the function of prepositions, prepositional phrases, and preposition idioms.

Noun phrases are groups of words which act as nouns.
A *gerund phrase* consists of a participle (verb+ing or verb+ed) and its modifiers acting as a noun. Gerunds show tense and voice.
1. Fran hates doing her laundry. direct object
2. Having learned to speak Spanish qualified Jennifer as an interpreter. subject
An *infinitive phrase* consists of to+verb and modifiers or object. Infinitives show tense and voice.
1. To have our own children was always our dream. subject
2. To have met President Reagan would have been a thrill. subject
3. His goal is to become a millionaire. predicate noun

To compare two nouns, use similar to or the same as; to contrast them use different from.
Common noun suffixes (-ance, -ant, -ence, -er, -ism, -ist, -ity, -ment, -ness, -tion, -ship) are often added to other parts of speech to form nouns. They are sometimes even added to other nouns to create new nouns. These suffixes cannot be added at random. When in doubt, check a dictionary.
Verb: commune
Noun: community
Adjective: different
Noun: difference
Noun: account
Noun: accountant
Adjectives, gerunds, infinitives, and prepositions sometimes act as nouns.

A *phrase* is a group of related words acting as one word-a noun, adjective, or adverb.
Infinitives are to+verb. An infinitive phrase is an infinitive plus any objects and modifiers. Infinitives can act as nouns, adjectives or adverbs.
Participles are verb+ing or verb+ed. Participial phrases can function as nouns, adjectives or adverbs. A participle in a phrase shows tense and voice.
When a participle has an object or modifiers and acts as a noun, it is a *gerund phrase*. When a participle has an object or modifiers and acts as an adjective, it is a participial phrase. When a participle has a subject and modifies an entire sentence, it is an absolute phrase.
A *prepositional phrase* consists of a preposition, its object and any modifiers. Prepositional phrases can act as adjectives or adverbs.
An *appositive phrase* identifies or defines the word it follows.

The sentence is the basic unit of communication in English. Parts of speech--*adjectives, adverbs, articles, conjunctions, nouns, pronouns, prepositions, verbs, and interjections*--identify the words which make up a sentence.
Nouns, verbs, adjectives, and adverbs perform essential functions in a sentence and provide the sentence with its content.
Two other parts of speech--conjunctions and prepositions--connect sentences to each other; and, within a sentence, they connect one part-- one idea or action--to another.
Some words function only as one part of speech. However, many words can function as two or more parts of speech.

Prepositions are connectors. They connect the words which follow them to the rest of the sentence. The most commonly used prepositions are listed below:
about above aboard across after against along among against around at before behind below beneath beside besides between beyond by despite down during except for from in inside into like near of off on out outside over past since through throughout to toward under underneath until up upon with within without
A preposition must be followed by a nominal--a noun, pronoun, gerund, noun phrase, or noun clause.
Prepositional phrases act as adjectives or adverbs.
Idiomatic Use of Prepositions - Some adjectives, nouns, and verbs are always followed by the same preposition--for example, afraid of, agree with.

A *pronoun* always refers back to a noun. That noun is the pronoun's antecedent. Example: She bought some (antecedent) furniture yesterday, but (pronoun) it hasn't arrived. Pronoun and antecedent must agree in number and gender.
Example: We were happy when our (antecedent) relatives came. It was great seeing (pronoun) them.
A *personal pronoun* refers to a person or thing. A personal pronoun can be a subject, an object, or a possessive. Personal pronouns usually change their form depending on if they are used as the subject or object of a sentence.
1st Person: I, we, me, us, mine, ours
2nd Person: you, yours
3rd Person: he, she, it, they, him, her, them, his, hers, theirs
Interrogative pronouns (who, whom, which, what, and whose) ask questions.
Relative pronouns (who, whom, which, that, whose) introduce adjective and noun clauses. The relative pronoun, what, introduces noun clauses only. Within an adjective or noun clause, the relative pronoun can function as a subject, object, or possessive. Relative pronouns of the -ever form (whatever, whichever, whoever, whomever) have an indefinite meaning: they do not refer back to a specific noun.

Describe the function of a sentence.

Describe demonstrative pronouns, reflexive pronouns, intensive pronouns, and reciprocal pronouns.

Describe the function of a verb.

Describe sentence structure.

Describe transitive and intransitive verbs.

Describe linking verbs.

Demonstrative pronouns (this/these, that/those) indicate distance.
This/these usually indicate nearness in time or space.
That/those usually indicate more distant time and space.
This/that are used with singular nouns. These/those are used with plural nouns.
When the exact quantity or identity of a person, idea or thing, is unknown, use an indefinite pronoun. Although most indefinite pronouns take singular verbs, a few indefinite pronouns take plural verbs and some can take either singular or plural.
Singular Verb: anybody, everyone, something
Plural Verb: few, many, several
Singular/Plural: most, some
Intensive/reflexive pronouns are made by adding -self, -selves to personal pronouns. For example: myself, ourselves. An intensive pronoun emphasizes the noun or pronoun that comes before it.
Example: Doug did the work himself.
A reflexive pronoun indicates that the subject and the object of an action are the same person. Example: Ed shot himself in the foot.
Reciprocal pronouns are each other, one another. They refer back to a compound or a plural subject to indicate a relationship.

An English sentence has two parts, the subject and the predicate. The *subject* identifies the topic of the sentence. The *predicate* comments on the topic. The subject must include a noun or a phrase or clause acting as a noun. The predicate must include a verb.
Example: Fred and his wife like to cook.
Subject: Fred and his wife
Predicate: like to cook.

The purpose of a sentence refers to its function. Does the sentence state a fact or an opinion? Does it ask a question? Does it give a command? Does it show excitement?
Declarative – A declarative sentence makes a statement and ends with a period. Example: Animals have their own language. states a fact
Interrogative – An interrogative sentence asks a question and ends with a question mark. Example: Do animals have their own language?
Imperative – An imperative sentence gives a command or makes a request; it ends with a period or an exclamation point. Example: Come with me.
Exclamatory – An exclamatory sentence shows sudden or strong feeling; it ends with an exclamation point. Example: How beautiful she is!

A sentence can be identified according to its structure: simple, compound, complex, or compound-complex.
Every *simple* sentence is an independent clause, which contains a subject and verb, expresses one complete thought, and is grammatically independent. Example: It rained yesterday.
A *compound* sentence has two or more independent clauses joined by a semicolon(;) or by a comma and a coordinating conjunction, such as and, but, or. Example: She likes to eat fruit, and I like to eat vegetables.
A *complex* sentence has one independent clause and at least one dependent clause. The dependent clause is introduced by a relative pronoun (who, which, that, etc.) or a subordinating conjunction (although, because, when, etc.). Example: Because I like to drink milk, my bones are very strong.
A *compound-complex* sentence has two or more independent clauses plus one or more dependent clauses. Example: The plane arrived and we took off, because we were already late.

Verbs state what happens (such as eat or run) or describe a state of being (such as be or appear). All verbs indicate time (hear, heard, will hear; is, was, will be).
All verbs need a subject identifying who or what is acting or being- I think; I am.
Some verbs also have a direct object (He eats meat).
Verbs have five forms: *base form, past tense, past participle, present participle, infinitive.*
Regular verbs form the past tense and the past participle by adding -ed to the base form of the verb (kick, kicked, kicked; walk, walked, walked).
Irregular verbs form the past tense and past participle in many different ways: buy, bought, bought; see, saw, seen.

Linking verbs do not express action; linking verbs express a state of being. Linking verbs are followed by nouns or adjectives. See examples below:
John was a doctor.
The grapefruit is too sour.
Here is a list of frequently used linking verbs:
Be (am, is, are, was, were, being, been) is the most common linking verb. Sense-related verbs (feel, look, smell, sound, taste) also act as linking verbs.
Some other verbs (appear, become, grow, seem) can also act as linking verbs. An adjective following a linking verb describes the subject. Example: This fruit is really mushy.
A noun following a linking verb renames the subject. See example: He is a doctor.
Some verbs (appear, become, feel, grow, look, smell, sound, and taste) are either linking verbs or action verbs, depending on their meaning in a sentence.
Linking verb: Mary grew ill.
Action verbs: We grew tomatoes.

Action verbs tell what happens. They are either transitive (buy, kick, see) or intransitive (walk, fall).
A *transitive verb* is an action verb requiring a direct object (noun, pronoun, noun phrase or clause) to complete its meaning. A transitive verb can also have an indirect object or an objective complement. See examples below:
Mary showed the ring.
Mary showed his mom the ring.
The country elected him President.
An *intransitive verb* is an action verb which can not accept a direct object. An intransitive verb is followed by an adverbial modifier-an adverb, a prepositional phrase-or nothing at all. See examples below:
Fred jumped high.
Fred jumped in the puddle.
Fred jumped.

Describe simple present, simple past, and future verb tenses.

Describe present perfect, past perfect, and future perfect verb tenses.

Describe present, past, and future continuous verb tenses.

Describe present, past, and future perfect continuous verb tenses.

Discuss active vs. passive verbs.

Describe auxiliary verbs.

The *present perfect* tense emphasizes the completion of an action in the very recent past. Example: I have just purchased a necklace.
The *present perfect tense* can also indicate an action begun in the past and continued up to the present moment. See example below:
Sam has lived at the same house for ten years.
The *past perfect* indicates how two finished actions are related in time. The first completed action uses the past perfect while the second action uses the simple past. Example: Before he went blind, Milton had written Paradise Lost.
Future perfect indicates an action to be finished before a future time. Example: I will have finished the book before I take the exam.

Verbs change form to agree with the subject of the action and to indicate the time or tense of the action. Verb tenses can be categorized as simple or perfect. Each of these tenses has a continuous form.
Simple present tense expresses habitual or repeated actions, general truths, future actions, literary or historic present, and states or qualities of being. In statements, do/does expresses emphasis. See examples below:
Susie exercises on Thursdays and Fridays. habitual action
Fred is a doctor. linking verb--state of being
Simple past tense expresses finished actions. Did in statements expresses emphasis. See examples below.
World War II ended in 1945. finished action
Benedict Arnold began as a loyal American, but later he did betray his country. emphasis
Future tense expresses actions or conditions occurring in the future. Simple present tense with an adverb of time can indicate future.
She will see it next week. future tense
The insurance coverage ends next month. simple present

The *present perfect continuous* emphasizes that an action which began in the past will continue into the future. Example: Arlene has been studying music for three years; she still has one more year to go.
The *future perfect continuous* indicates an action continuing until some specific time in the future. Example: He will have been attending school for nineteen years by the time he graduates.
The *past perfect continuous* emphasizes that the first action continued right up to the time of the second action. Example: By the year 2050, people will have been living on Mars for a decade or more.

The *present continuous* expresses ongoing but temporary or future actions. See examples below:
I am riding a bicycle now. ongoing temporary action
She is flying to Australia next summer. future action
Past continuous usually expresses an action in progress at the time of another past action. Example: Sheila was attending a class when the fire alarm went off.
Future continuous expresses a future action. Example: She will be driving to Maine next year.

Auxiliary verbs (helping verbs and modals) convey important information, but they never work alone. They must combine with a main verb.
Helping verbs combine with a main verb to identify verb tense, number and voice and to introduce questions and form negatives. The helping verbs are be, do, have, will.
Be (am/is/are/was/were/been) helps make the continuous forms and the passive voice.
Continuous forms:
be (am/is/are/was/were/been) + present participle + (verb+ing)
Example:
The girl is running. present continuous
The girl was running. past continuous
The girl has been running. present perfect continuous
The girl had been running. past perfect continuous
Is the girl running? present continuous
Was the girl running? past continuous
Has the girl been running? present perfect continuous
Had the girl been running? past perfect continuous

In an active voice sentence, the subject is the actor. In a passive voice sentence, the opposite is true: the subject is the receiver or the object of the action.
Examples:
Active voice: Mary rocked the baby.
Passive voice: The baby was rocked by Mary.
Only transitive verbs use the passive voice.
The passive voice is formed by using be (am, is, are, was, were, being, been) + past participle.

Describe verb usage in subjunctive sentences.

Describe verb usage in conditional sentences.

Describe verb patterns.

Describe more detailed verb usage in subjunctive sentences.

Discuss capitalization rules for proper nouns.

Describe verbs ending in "ed" or "ing."

Verb tense is the key to writing correct conditional and subjunctive sentences.

Conditional sentences express the idea that one situation depends on another. In a conditional sentence, the situation in the independent clause 'your summer begins in January' depends on the situation in the conditional, or 'if,' clause--if you live in Brazil. If, when, whether, and unless introduce conditional sentences. Conditional independent clause: If you live in Brazil, your summer begins in January.

Conditional sentences which express facts, general truths, or habitual actions use the simple present tense in both clauses.
Examples:
If the moon is full, it is hard to see the stars.
When the temperature rises above 85 degrees, we turn on the air conditioning.
Conditional sentences which predict probable actions use the simple present tense in the conditional, or 'if,' clause. The independent clause uses 'will' or a modal.
Example: If it rains tonight, we will cancel the party.

The *subjunctive mood* is used in formal written English to express conditions contrary to fact, wishes, requests, or demands. A key to writing accurate subjunctive sentences is to ignore normal rules of tense and number.

'Condition contrary to fact' describes a situation that does not exist now, never existed, and is unlikely ever to exist; for example, if Thomas Jefferson were alive today or if Thomas Jefferson had been alive during the Civil War.

The 'if clause' uses the past tense; the independent clause uses would/could/might and the base form of the verb. Example: If I were a billionaire, I would buy all the TV networks.

The 'if clause' uses past perfect; the independent clause uses a would/could/might and the present perfect tense. Example: If I had been born in 1900, I would have sailed around the world.

Sentences expressing wishes use the subjunctive in the 'that clause.'

For present tense wishes, use were, the simple past tense, or would/could/might and the simple form of the verb in the 'that clause.'
Example: I wish that the semester were over now.
When a wish is about the past, use the past perfect or would/could/might and the present perfect in the 'that clause.' Example:
He wished that the semester had ended before he ran out of money.
Ask, demand, insist, move, recommend, suggest, and urge followed by 'that clauses' use the simple form of the verb to express both present and past tense. Example: The president asks that everyone work together.

Some verbs are followed by *verbals* (gerunds or infinitives) according to a rigid pattern--want to go but enjoy going. Listed below are the five different patterns.
1. Verb + Infinitive - Napoleon chose to marry Josephine.
2. Verb + Gerund - He is enjoying playing tennis these days.
3. Verb + Infinitive or Verb + Gerund - The boy loves going to school.
4. Verb + Object + Verb - She helped him build a house.
5. Verb + Object + Infinitive - They wanted us to teach them to read Spanish.

When used as adjectives, the past participle (verb+ed) and the present participle (verb+ing) of some verbs have very different meanings.
Psychological verbs (interest, bore, amuse, etc.) describe emotions or moods. When their participles are used as adjectives, they follow the rules below.
The past participle (verb+ed) describes the person's mental state or inner feelings: the tired student.
The present participle (verb+ing) describes the person or thing which causes the mental state or feelings: the tiring exercises or the tiring speaker.
The most common psychological verbs are: amuse, disappoint, flatter, overwhelm, annoy, disgust, frighten, reassure, bore, encourage, horrify, satisfy, charm, excite, inspire, surprise, confuse, fascinate, interest.
When the participles of action verbs (burn, blow, melt, etc.) are used as adjectives, they follow the rules below.
The past participle (verb+ed) indicates a completed action—melted snow.
The present participle (verb+ing) emphasizes an ongoing process—melting snow.
Action completed: blown hair, boiled water.
Ongoing process: blowing hair, boiling water.

Capitalize *proper nouns* and words formed from proper nouns.
- Capitalize names of *particular persons*: **G**eorge **B**ush, **J**esus **C**hrist.
- Capitalize names of *particular places*, including continents, countries, states, cities, and streets: **A**sia, **C**anada, **W**ashington, **N**ew **Y**ork **C**ity, **P**ennsylvania **A**venue.
- Capitalize names of *particular things*, such as special organizations, holidays, historical events, races and religions, languages, business product brand names, and other particular things such as planets, documents, and monuments: **S**enate, **M**other's **D**ay, **C**ivil **W**ar, **E**nglishman, **C**atholic, **F**ord truck, **V**enus, **D**eclaration of **I**ndependence, and **W**ashington **M**emorial.
- Capitalize words *formed from proper nouns*, such as abbreviations of proper nouns and proper adjectives: **CPA**, **E**nglish.
- Capitalize a common noun or adjective only when it is a *part of a proper name*: **L**ouisiana **S**tate **U**niversity

Describe miscellaneous capitalization rules.

Describe capitalization rules for titles of persons.

Describe parallelism.

Describe noun-pronoun agreement in number.

Describe negation.

Describe pronoun-noun agreement in gender.

Capitalize *titles of persons*.
- Capitalize titles when they are used *before a person's name* as part of the name: **P**resident Bush, **K**ing David
- Titles *following a name or used alone in place of a name* are not usually capitalized unless used in direct address: the **P**resident of the United States
- Capitalize *family-relationship words* when they are used *before a person's name* and when used *alone in place of the name*: **U**ncle Mike came over for dinner. Hello, **D**ad.

Capitalize the titles of works.
- Capitalize the first and last words and all important words in the titles of *books, magazines, newspapers, poems, stories, plays, and works of art*: **G**one **W**ith the **W**ind (book), **N**ew **Y**ork **T**imes (newspaper).
- Capitalize the *first word of every sentence* (including quoted sentences). Patrick Henry said "**G**ive me liberty or give me death."
- Capitalize the pronoun I.
- Capitalize the *first word in every line of poetry*, whether or not the word begins a sentence. See example below:

For though from out our bourne of Time and Place
    The flood may bear me far,
I hope to see my Pilot face to face
    When I have crossed the bar.
                 - Tennyson

A pronoun must agree with its antecedent in *number*. If the antecedent is singular, the pronoun referring to it must be singular; if the antecedent is plural, the pronoun referring to it must be plural.
- Use *singular* pronouns to refer to the singular indefinite pronouns: *each, either, neither, one, everyone, everybody, no one, nobody, anyone, anybody, someone, somebody*.
Example: *Each* of the students bought *their* own lunch. (incorrect)
        Each of the students bought *his* own lunch. (correct)
- Use plural nouns to refer to the plural indefinite pronouns: *both, few, several, many*. Example: *Both* were within *their* boundaries.
- The indefinite pronouns *some, any, none, all, most* may be referred to by *singular* or *plural* pronouns, depending on the sense of the sentence.
Examples: *Some* of the children have misplaced *their* toy. (plural)
Some of the carpet has lost *its* nap. (singular)
- Pronouns that refer to compound antecedents joined by *and* are usually plural. Example: Bill and Joe cook *their* own meals.

When a sentence contains a series of items, all the items should be in parallel form. Keeping all phrases and clauses in the same form creates parallelism by clarifying the relationship among the parts of the sentence.
Incorrect: I like running and to swim. (This sentence is not parallel; "running" and "to swim" are not in the same form.
Sentences can be corrected by putting both words in the same form.
Correct: I like running and swimming. (Both words are now in an "–ing" form.
Parallel grammatical structure is important for clear and concise sentences.

A pronoun agrees with its antecedent in gender.
- Antecedents of *masculine* gender (male sex) are referred to by *he, him, his*.
- Antecedents of *feminine* gender (female sex) are referred to by *she, her, hers*.
- Antecedents of *neuter* gender (no sex) are referred to by *it, its*.
- Antecedents of *common* gender (sex not known) are referred to by *he, him, his*. It is understood that the masculine pronouns include both male and female.
- Antecedents that are names of animals are generally referred to by the neuter pronouns unless the writer wishes to indicate special interest in the animal, in which case the masculine pronouns are often used. When a feminine role is naturally suggested, the feminine pronouns are used.

Negation is the process that turns an affirmative statement (I am the walrus) into its opposite denial (I am not the walrus). Nouns as well as verbs can be grammatically negated, by the use of a negative adjective (There is no walrus), a negative pronoun (Nobody is the walrus), or a negative adverb (I never was the walrus). The negative particles are not and no; the negative particle is placed after the auxiliary verb in a sentence.
In English, negation for most verbs other than be and have, or verb phrases in which be, have or do already occur, requires the recasting of the sentence using the dummy auxiliary verb do, which adds little to the meaning of the negative phrase, but serves as a place to attach the negative particles not, or its contracted form -n't, to:
I have a walrus.
I don't have a walrus. (the most common way in contemporary English.)
I do not see the walrus.
I am not seeing the walrus.
I have not seen the walrus.
The verb do also follows this rule, and therefore requires a second instance of itself in order to be marked for negation:
"The walrus doesn't do tricks " not "The walrus doesn't tricks."

Discuss word usage.

Discuss points to keep in mind while writing an exam essay.

Discuss uses for transitional words and phrases.

Describe various types of paragraphs that can make up the essay body.

1. Clearly announce your position in response to the specified topic and establish the structure of the essay
2. Organize what you plan to write and follow it closely.
3. Be direct and to the point.
4. Provide examples and clear explanations
5. Avoid generalizations.
6. Use transitional phrases to get from one point to another; develop a logical flow between ideas.
7. Use variety in sentence structure; follow rules of standard written English.
8. Save time for revising and editing.

Word usage, or *diction*, refers to the use of words with meanings and forms that are appropriate for the context and structure of a sentence. A common error in word usage occurs when a word's meaning does not fit the context of the sentence.
Incorrect: Susie likes chips better then candy.
Correct: Susie likes chips better than candy.
Incorrect: The cat licked it's colt.
Correct: the cat licked its colt.
Commonly misused words include *than/then, it's/its, they/their/they're, your/you're, except/accept,* and *affect/effect.*

Explanation: give examples, facts, and details
Compare and contrast: discusses how things are similar or different
Chronological: arranged according to timing
Spatial: arranged according to location
Emphasis: arranged in order of importance
Cause and effect: arranged from effect to cause or cause to effect
Problem/solution: arranged according to issues and solutions
Topical: arranged according to topics discussed

Transitional words and phrases can be used to:
1. To add ideas: again; furthermore; besides; too; also
2. To compare or contrast: likewise; yet; however; although
3. To prove: because; since; obviously
4. To show exceptions: yet; however; occasionally
5. To show time: soon; finally; next; then; later
6. To show effect: consequently; thus; therefore
7. To emphasize: obviously; certainly; indeed
8. To give examples: for example; to demonstrate; to illustrate
9. To conclude: thus; consequently; therefore

GUARANTEED TO IMPROVE YOUR TEST SCORE

"Effective, Affordable, Guaranteed"

At Mometrix, we think differently about tests. We believe you can perform better on your exam by implementing a few critical strategies and focusing your study time on what's most important. With so many demands on your time, you probably don't have months to spend preparing for an exam that holds the key to your future. Our team of testing experts devote hours upon hours to painstakingly review piles of content and boil it all down to the critical concepts that are most likely to be on your exam. We do a lot of work cutting through the fluff to give you what you need the most to perform well on the exam. But you don't have to take our word for it; here is what some of our customers have to say:

We offer study materials for over 1000 different standardized exams, including:

Teacher Certification Exams	**College Entrance Exams**
Insurance Exams	**Medical/Nursing Exams**
Dental Exams	**Financial Exams**
Graduate & Professional Exams	**Military Exams**

For questions about bulk discounts or ordering through your company/institution, please contact our Institutional Sales Department at 888-248-1219 or sales@mometrix.com.

Visit www.MometrixCatalog.com for our full list of products and services.

Information in this publication is included for utilitarian purposes only and does not constitute an endorsement by Mometrix of any particular point of view.

Mometrix Media LLC publishes a variety of unofficial educational materials.

All trademarks are property of their respective trademark owners.

Made in USA